Voltaire

PHILOSOPHICAL LETTERS

Or, Letters Regarding the English Nation

Voltaire

PHILOSOPHICAL LETTERS

Or, Letters Regarding the English Nation

EDITED, WITH AN INTRODUCTION, BY
John Leigh

TRANSLATED BY
Prudence L. Steiner

Hackett Publishing Company, Inc.
Indianapolis/Cambridge

Copyright © 2007 by Hackett Publishing Company, Inc.

For further information, please address:

Hackett Publishing Company, Inc.
P.O. Box 44937
Indianapolis, IN 46244-0937

www.hackettpublishing.com

Cover design by Abigail Coyle
Text design and composition by Jennifer Plumley
Printed at Edward Brothers, Inc.

Library of Congress Cataloging-in-Publication Data

Voltaire, 1694–1778.
  [Lettres philosophiques. English]
  Philosophical letters, or, Letters regarding the English nation /
Voltaire ; edited, with an introduction, by John Leigh ; translated by
Prudence L. Steiner.
       p. cm.
  Includes bibliographical references.
  ISBN-13: 978-0-87220-882-7
  ISBN-13: 978-0-87220-881-0 (pbk.)
  1. Imaginary letters. 2. Philosophy, Modern—18th century. 3. Great
Britain—Civilization—18th century. I. Leigh, John, 1969– II. Steiner,
Prudence L. III. Title. IV. Title: Philosophical letters. V. Title: Letters
regarding the English nation.

  PQ2086.L4E5 2007
  848'.509—dc22

                                                    2006034696

∞

vi   Contents

CONTENTS

INTRODUCTION

Towards the end of the thirteenth of his *Philosophical Letters*, Voltaire momentarily stops to exclaim:

> What am I saying! All the books of modern philosophers together will not cause as much trouble in the world as did the Franciscan monks in their disputes about the proper shapes of their sleeves and hoods. (p. 45)

Voltaire's promise that all books by or about philosophers are destined to be safely inconsequential is no doubt calculated in part to disarm and neutralize the critics he knew to be circling around this, his own work. But if he were hoping that the philosophical discussions entertained by the book might be ignored or dismissed, he would be disappointed. First published in 1733 and 1734, a few years after Voltaire left England in 1728, the *Philosophical Letters*, or the *Letters upon the English Nation* (for it was published in both English and French), saw numerous editions throughout the eighteenth century and became one of the bestsellers of the age. It also landed Voltaire in serious trouble. The publication of the "Philosophical, Political, Critical, Poetical, Heretical, and Diabolical Letters" (to give it the expanded title Voltaire would later cheerfully bestow on the fateful book) forced him out of Paris and to Cirey, on the borders of France and Lorraine, then a small independent Duchy not quite annexed to France.[1]

Characteristically, even as he is assuring the reader that philosophers are perfectly harmless, Voltaire cannot resist a remark at the expense of Christianity, and in particular, the self-important and fractious Franciscans. Throughout the text, Voltaire's unsparing criticism of the Church, and his vilification of Church views and policies—its opposition to inoculation, refusal to provide actors a Christian burial, and intolerance and complacency—invites trouble. But Voltaire dared also to praise England, France's traditional enemy. This was bound to hurt even those French sensibilities not already pricked by the attacks on religion.

Throughout the *Philosophical Letters*, as in the example above, Voltaire moves between meek courtesies, careful elucidation, and mordantly satirical observations within one breath. He sometimes concludes his letters by retreating into disingenuous prose, in which his apparent ignorance barely disguises the satirical intent. A beautiful example surfaces at the end of the tenth letter, where Voltaire purports to be beset by uncertainty:

> I, however, do not know which is the more useful to the State: a nobleman in a powdered wig who knows exactly when the king arises and when he retires, and who gives himself airs of greatness while he plays the slave in the antechamber of a minister, or a merchant who enriches his country, who sends orders from his counting house to Surat and Cairo, and contributes to the well-being of the world. (p. 32)

As Voltaire turns his attention from the nobleman to the merchant, his syntax and vocabulary change slightly. When describing the nobleman, some additional detail (he wears a *powdered* wig and knows *exactly* when the king rises) perhaps helps to evoke his superfluous existence. When describing the activity of the merchant, Voltaire sheds adjectives and adverbs and, appropriately, his style becomes more economical.

Voltaire's apparent uncertainty here and elsewhere appears to empower his readers, who will duly make up their own minds and come to their own judgments, rather than simply assenting to those of the author. He is, of course, pressing home a serious and controversial point about the respective values of life at court and commerce, but he invites us to take possession of the argument.

In writing his letters from England to France, Voltaire places seemingly equivalent values in the balance, before proceeding to tip that balance delicately but inexorably one way. Just as he pretends to vacillate between the nobleman and the merchant at the end of the tenth letter, so at the start of the fourteenth letter he appears to juxtapose alternative philosophical systems as if they were equally viable, those of René Descartes and Isaac Newton, rival French and English thinkers. Voltaire describes their mutually exclusive cosmologies as though they were regional differences. Voltaire's tone is as innocuous as that of a French tourist in London writing home to say that the English drive on the other side of the road from the French. These arbitrary differences seem equally valid and plausible.

> A Frenchman arriving in London finds changes in philosophy as in other matters. He left a universe that was filled; he discovers the

CHRONOLOGY

Events	Selected Works of Voltaire
1694	**Born François-Marie Arouet in Paris** Bank of England founded	
1697	Birth of William Hogarth	
1702	Accession of Queen Anne to English throne	
1703	Tsar Peter the Great founds St. Petersburg	
1704	Battle of Blenheim Death of John Locke	
1707	Union of England and Scotland ratified	
1712	Birth of Jean-Jacques Rousseau	
1714	Death of Queen Anne. Accession of George I	
1715	Death of Louis XIV. Regency of the Duc d'Orléans	
1716	**Voltaire exiled from Paris on account of a satire**	
1717	**Voltaire in the Bastille**	
1718	**Adopts the name Voltaire**	Voltaire's first success, a tragedy, *Œdipe*
1721	Montesquieu, *Lettres persanes*	
1726	**Beaten by the Chevalier de Rohan, Voltaire in Bastille again. Travels to England**	
1727	George I dies. Accession of George II	*Essay upon Epic Poetry*

1728		*La Henriade* published
1731	Prévost, *Le philosophe anglais ou l'histoire de M. Cleveland*	*La mort de Mlle. Lecouvreur*
1732		*Zaïre*, a play dedicated to an English merchant, Fawkener, succeeds
1733		*Philosophical Letters* published in London *La mort de César*
1734	**Settles in Cirey (in Champagne) with mistress, Mme du Châtelet**	
1736		A poem, *Le Mondain*
1738		*Eléments de la philosophie de Newton*
1741	War of the Austrian Succession (until 1748)	*Mahomet* first performed
1743	**Elected a Fellow of the Royal Society**	
1744	Death of Alexander Pope	
1745	**Appointed Royal Historiographer by Louis XV**	
1746	**Elected to the Académie française**	
1747		*Zadig*, the first of Voltaire's short stories published
1749	Birth of Goethe	
1750	**Death of Mme. du Châtelet Voltaire at court of Frederick the Great, Potsdam**	*Memnon*
1751	Publication of *Encyclopédie* (until 1772)	*Le siècle de Louis XIV*
1752	Britain adopts Gregorian Calendar	*Micromégas*
1753	**Voltaire arrested in Frankfurt by Frederick's men** Foundation of British Museum	

1755	Lisbon earthquake	
1756		*Poème sur le désastre de Lisbonne*
1756	Seven Years War (until 1763)	*Essai sur les mœurs*
1759		*Candide*
1759-78	**Voltaire in Ferney (on Swiss/ French border)**	
1761	Rousseau, *Julie* Diderot, *Eloge de Richardson*	
1763	Calas affair	*Traité sur la tolérance*
1764		*Dictionnaire philosophique*
1765		*Homélies prononcées à Londres*
1766	Rousseau in England	*Examen important de milord Bolingbroke*
1767		*L'Ingénu*
1768	Sterne, *A sentimental journey through France and Italy*	
1775		*Histoire de Jenni ou le sage et l'athée (par M. Sherloc)*
1776	Death of Louis XV. Accession of Louis XVI Declaration of American Independence	
1778	**Death of Voltaire in Paris**	*Irène*
1782	Laclos, *Les Liaisons dangereuses*	
1784	**First volumes of Voltaire's first Complete Works directed by Beaumarchais**	
1786	Death of Frederick the Great	
1791	**Transferral to Pantheon**	

void; in Paris, they imagine a universe composed of vortices of subtle matter; in London none of this. [. . .] In Paris the earth is shaped like a melon; in London, it is flattened at both ends. (p. 47)

Voltaire's style initially does justice to both viewpoints, by suggesting not only that French and English perceptions of the world are at variance, but that the world is in fact different in London and Paris. But, of course, Voltaire is under no illusion that one view is right and the other wrong. Expounding Newton's science with enthusiasm, Voltaire duly kicks the Parisian melon out of play. He destroys Descartes' flawed cosmology with relish, but he does so from behind the apparently anodyne form of the travel account.

From the very first words of the *Philosophical Letters*, the rather tentative "It seemed to me . . . ," (Letter 1, p. 1) to the end of the last letter in which Voltaire describes his own mind as "limited" (Letter 25, p. 122), after sustaining a relentless attack on Pascal, another influential French thinker, Voltaire underplays and disguises the satirical sharpness of his remarks, burying a philosophical treatise in a set of seemingly private, often anecdotal observations.

Because the philosophical insights and discussions take the form of observations recorded in letters, Voltaire can strike a friendly, informal pose. Voltaire, or more properly perhaps, the affable persona he constructs for these letters, sometimes tells us what he has just done: "I have told you a little about their philosophers" (Letter 22, p. 91). And he occasionally throws in the odd, perhaps redundant comment about what he is trying to do: "I will tell you (if I can do so, concisely) the little I have been able to understand of these sublime ideas" (Letter 15, p. 51). Voltaire need not utter these words—indeed, they only add to the "verbiage" he is purporting to avoid—but he knows that his imprint on the text is crucial to its success. He is sufficiently relaxed to admit that he has in mind "several authors whose names escape me here" and not to bother looking up the names, relying instead on his own memory and wit.

When Voltaire comes to Newton, he acknowledges that this thinker's genius is practically divine, but humble appreciation of Newton's gifts does not preclude a bold and impatient desire to learn his ideas. Miraculous as Newton's accomplishments may be, his genius can be comprehended if not emulated. It is a shame that, unlike many writers and philosophers in the eighteenth century, Voltaire never seems to have assumed the role of a teacher. On the evidence of the *Philosophical Letters*, he has a gift for condensing and imparting complex ideas. Indeed, it was Voltaire who first made famous the story of Newton's apple, which Newton's niece had told him. Voltaire immediately realized the value of a "bite-sized" anecdote.

From the very first letter, Voltaire crafts the persona of a companionable writer, a man who is at once curious and reasonable—and, of course, amusing. He relies exclusively on his own resources, and his judgments are entirely his own. He neither concurs with nor dissents from previous verdicts on England. He does not acknowledge any previous traveler (either French or foreign), nor does he quote any literary sources. He therefore seems approachable, and the wisdom he has achieved attainable.

By the time the *Letters* were published, Voltaire was well-known and yet, in essence, unknown. He was already famous as a playwright and a poet. Prior to his arrival in England, he had come to the attention of the nation's foremost poet, Alexander Pope, whose portrait Voltaire says he saw in as many as twenty houses in England (Letter 23, p. 93). In 1724 or 1725, Voltaire's portrait had been painted by Nicolas de Largillière, who was important enough to have painted King James II of England and his consort, Mary of Modena. Voltaire was right to look pleased in his picture. Yet although his face may have become widely known through such portraits, few people were privy to what Voltaire really thought. To begin with, Voltaire was a name contrived by a man once called François Marie Arouet, who did not want his father's surname and, indeed, did not believe that Arouet senior could possibly be his father.

Thus, although Voltaire is strikingly approachable, he remains ultimately elusive. In this first-person text, Voltaire reveals as little as possible about himself. His history, identity, and motivation are effaced. Voltaire chooses not to tell us how he came to be in England, nor what he is doing there, nor why. The mystery perhaps results in a semblance of objectivity. Voltaire does not distract his readers with information that might explain a particular stance or point of view. He is simply a Frenchman who finds himself in England, it seems, to satisfy his avowed curiosity.

From the outset this Frenchman seems to be a paragon of politeness and reasonableness as he meets a Quaker, the representative of a minority religion that is merely tolerated in England and elsewhere overwhelmingly ignored. Voltaire's tactic in beginning a book about the English nation in this way seems both perverse and provocative. Perverse because books about England would customarily begin with descriptions of the Royal Palaces or a historical overview or the weather. Provocative because Voltaire takes pleasure in pushing a minority figure from the margins into the center of attention, and for no fewer than four letters. In beginning his account of the English nation by speaking with the exponent of a minority religion, Voltaire—with an eye to the suffocating orthodoxies of French religion—refuses to generalize about the English and England.

The opening letter is superbly crafted, as it registers the shock of novelty reverberating in both directions. Voltaire, beholding the Quaker, claims never to have seen such a noble countenance. The Quaker, in turn, has never encountered a Frenchman characterized by such curiosity. The meeting initially shows Voltaire to be the more dynamic character. Not only has he sought the Quaker out, but Voltaire's gestures and movements opposite this intractable older man make the Quaker seem rather gruff and forbidding. Voltaire's prose, with its succession of paired adjectives, seems to measure his own equipoise and assurance.

However, the physical contrast is deceptive. Intellectually, the positions are soon reversed. It is the Quaker who is mentally agile and the persona of Voltaire who turns out to be inflexible and immobile; the source of satire rapidly becomes its target. After the deferential posturing of the Frenchman, it is disappointing that, when the Quaker reveals that he is not baptized, Voltaire loses his temper and starts swearing (in English, we assume, although it is not clear in which language the dialogue is transacted). These words, at odds with his polite gestures, signal a reversal. Henceforward, the Frenchman seems the more unreasonable of the two gentlemen.

By the eleventh letter, Voltaire acknowledges that the tables are truly turned: "In truth we are strange people!" (Letter 11, p. 35), he says of the French with some exasperation. Even in this exclamation, there remains a first-person plural "we" that includes the writer and his reader, but at other moments in the text, Voltaire slips into identification with England, and his fellow French citizens become "you" rather than "we." Voltaire thus catches us out. The *Letters* initially create the illusion that we can trust the person who has written them, but as he obsequiously bows towards the Quaker, Voltaire is also "wrong-footing" the reader.

In short, Voltaire keeps us on our toes. This means that the text is more fun to read, and Voltaire would not have apologized for that. But perhaps the surprises, twists, and ironies in the *Letters* also lend support to a Voltairean conviction about the way we should approach books. The author and reader ideally meet one another halfway. As Voltaire says in the preface to his *Dictionnaire philosophique*, "the most useful books are those to which the reader contributes half." In other words, it is not up to the author to make all the running for the benefit of an inert reader. Nor should authors expect their readers to struggle in the dark without some guidance. In the fifteenth letter, then, as Voltaire sets out to explain the Newtonian system of attraction, he warns us in a telling phrase: "in philosophical matters one must be wary both of what one understands too easily and of what one does not understand at all" (Letter 15, p. 51).

Voltaire, true to the ambitions of the typical Enlightenment writer, trains a discerning eye over the irrational terrain of the ancien régime, and his satire of the cruel absurdities propagated in France is memorable. But, just as importantly, he also warns us of the difficulties with which enlightenment is won and the dangers of coming to conclusions too quickly.

Sometimes Voltaire serves us up a maxim that is neat and circumscribed, seductively simple but not simplistic. For instance, his tribute to the religious freedom enjoyed in England is expressed in a particularly memorable line: "An Englishman, being a free man, goes to Heaven by whatever path he chooses" (Letter 5, p. 15). But it is easy to forget that Voltaire immediately follows that statement with a qualification that is typically sprightly and ironic: The easiest route to making one's fortune is the highway up through the Church of England, a fact that is responsible for numerous conversions (Letter 5, p. 15). As is so often the case in the satire of the *Letters*, the determining and driving force of financial interest is uppermost.

On occasion, of course, Voltaire does simplify, unduly and brilliantly. He enjoys telescoping complicated historical developments into sudden epiphanies. The shock of Newton's advent is registered in a few simple words: "This man has come" (Letter 16, p. 60). Newton was, after all, born on Christmas Day. Voltaire resorts to the hushed, reverential rhythms of biblical narrative. Voltaire had the dramatist's ability to compress an action into a single space and limited time, to squeeze a narrative into short sections of a dozen syllables, and to lend a voice to an array of different figures. English merchants fund Prince Eugene's campaign "in half an hour." Even the abstractions of mathematical and physical science are imaginatively placed in the mouths of the philosophers. Voltaire knows that Descartes and Newton never met, but he arranges a hypothetical encounter in which he imagines Descartes' response to someone who prophesies Newton (Letter 16, p. 59). Descartes becomes John the Baptist to the Messianic Newton. Having earlier ventriloquized Descartes, Voltaire is happy to pose a question or two of Pascal, in a hypothetical mode in the twenty-fifth letter. Shakespeare's impact is likewise that of a thunderbolt: "He created the theatre," says Voltaire.

In moving between the two nations, Voltaire encourages us to view the world as a set of analogies and antitheses. Frequently, he makes comparisons that are serviceable approximations for his French readers. Indeed, as he explicitly says in Letter 21, "I know nothing more useful, for the purposes of improving tastes, than the comparison of those great geniuses who have worked in the same areas." (p. 83)

He is quite happy to draw on the sort of comparative schema by which eighteenth-century travel writers regularly help out their readers.2 Thus Swift is, with plenty of reservations, the "English Rabelais"; Pope is accordingly praised as "the Boileau of England," and Congreve vaunted as the English Molière (Letter 24, p. 98). These approximations always implicitly pay tribute to the French component in the comparison, a stable referent against which novelty may be measured. Voltaire is thoroughly versed in and indebted to the French geniuses who dominated the seventeenth century, or "the century of Louis XIV," as he would call it, which is an imperishable touchstone for him.3 Voltaire considers that the great and durable works are those that transcend local particularities and can be translated universally. However, the comparative approach falters when Voltaire tries to describe to his French readers the experience of seeing and reading Shakespeare. Voltaire recognizes genius without being able to apprehend it. Convenient as this equitable to-ing and fro-ing across the Channel may be, it is also illusory. For Newton, as we have seen, eclipses Descartes almost totally, while Shakespeare does not turn out to be the counterpart of Corneille, as alleged, but embodies a much more violent, almost unaccountable and virtually untranslatable force. The savagery and popularity of Shakespeare confirmed for many French people their suspicions that the English were a beef-eating, bloodthirsty lot. Voltaire's lines on the "brilliant monsters" and "barbaric genius" of Shakespeare may seem almost heretical to us now, but Voltaire was one of the first, if not the first, to appreciate Shakespeare, whose unkempt genius was beginning to be appreciated just as the French were abandoning their manicured gardens filled with topiaries and parterres for the freer picturesque landscapes of the English garden.

Nevertheless, the vision of the English that results from this text, for all its philosophical excitement and revelatory courage, yet chimes with typical, traditional French discourses on England. Voltaire does warn us against the comfort and complacency of sticking to clichés, thanks to the memorable prominence he lends to minor figures like the Quaker. Rather than talk of the English collectively, he prefers to look at individuals who are brilliantly particular and distinct. However refractory the Quaker may be, he is still an archetypically taciturn Englishman. He, too, confirms widely held suppositions about English character, such as pragmatism and reserve. The Quaker has also made his money through trade. The commercial robustness of England, as contrasted with the effete courtesies encouraged by a French society obsessed with gallantry, is a cliché. In the Quaker, Voltaire happens to meet an articulate, intelligent, and modest representative of the commercial class, whereas Jacques Rosbif, a character in Louis de Boissy's play *Le Français à Londres* (running in Paris while Voltaire was in London) exhibits a vulgar example of the rich, self-satisfied merchant. They are different versions of the same generic prototype.

Voltaire by and large refrains from making general remarks about the character of the English. However, when (from Letters 18 to 23) he discusses English writers, he selects quotations from their works which, while chiefly exemplifying their craft, happen also to illustrate and consolidate a traditional conception of the English character.

Voltaire selects, as his chief example of Shakespeare's art, Hamlet's soliloquy—"To be or not to be"—in which Hamlet is considering suicide. The example he chooses from Dryden is no less pessimistic:

> When I consider life, 'tis all a cheat
> Yet fool'd by hope, men favour the deceit.

When he comes to discuss his friend Pope, Voltaire selects a passage from his comic poem, *The Rape of the Lock*. Yet even here, he makes straight for the "gloomy cave of spleen" where an assortment of lugubrious figures is to be found. The quotations collectively convey the same melancholic attitudes. These fragments, once collected, amount to a quite bleak mosaic of English life. While Voltaire often chooses extracts from poetry or plays which, like Hamlet's soliloquy, are first-person intimations, perhaps as much an implicit testimony to Voltaire's view of England as a boldly individualistic culture, he also seems to place an unremitting, if tacit, emphasis on the joylessness of the English.

Voltaire discusses only the formal properties of these majestically gloomy passages, leaving the content to speak for itself. In the process, he conveys the message that the English are bilious. Voltaire imparts a familiar and unpalatable truth about the English, suggesting possibly that the dauntless hatred of life apparently common to many English writers is both a product of their freedom and a determinant of their art. The incidental or even subliminal quality of the extracts quoted helps to guarantee their force.

Nevertheless, if the English owe some of their achievements—and indeed their unhappiness—to idiosyncrasies reserved to an island race, there would appear to be very little that is not also available, at least potentially, to the French. Voltaire does not give the French the luxury of thinking that the English are an essentially different people. He avoids resorting to the sorts of "explanations" that would let the French off the hook. Indeed, Voltaire's descriptions of English political and cultural life ultimately give way to discussions of human nature and a wider philosophical credo to which Voltaire will remain loyal for years to come. In his long life and career, the *Philosophical Letters* occupies a relatively early position, but Voltaire is already "Voltairean" in this work.

Stylistically, many of the little tricks and jokes that Voltaire perfects several years later in his stories like *Candide* (1759) are already in evidence here. He is tremendously adept at yoking adjectives to nouns that are not quite ready for them; be it the "pious intentions" of clergymen (Letter 5, p. 15), the "dazzling folly" of military conquests (Letter 8, p. 24), Malebranche's "sublime illusions" (Letter 13, p. 42), or Shakespeare's "brilliant monstrosities" (Letter 18, p. 73). Most famously, Blaise Pascal is described as a "sublime misanthrope" (Letter 25, p. 101). No writer excels Voltaire in maneuvering such "combinations" into satirically operative positions. Sometimes, little adverbs also guarantee the satirical force of a statement. In the fifth letter, for example, Voltaire states that the Tory government's zeal "did not go much farther than occasionally breaking some windows in the heretical chapels" (Letter 5, p. 15). Within a few breaths, the convocation of the lower orders "rejoiced in the freedom to assemble, to debate controversies, and, from time to time, to burn a few heretical books, that is, books that attacked it" (the government) (Letter 5, p. 15). In each case, nonchalant, almost invisible adverbs—"occasionally," "from time to time,"—sharpen the ironic flavor of the statement by making Voltaire appear to approve behavior that seems eminently moderate: After all, books were burned and windows smashed only every now and again.

In the fourteenth letter, Voltaire remarks that Descartes, endowed with a fertile imagination, had considerable poetic powers. Indeed, Voltaire adds, he even composed some verses for the Queen of

Sweden that "to the honor of his memory, were never published."
The negative comes as a surprise, after Voltaire's apparent enthusi-
asm. Without explicitly saying so, he succeeds in telling us that
Descartes let himself down in writing this poetry.

In the sixth letter, Voltaire, always ready to oppose austerity of any
kind, marvels at the severity of the Presbyterians and their sanctifi-
cation of Sundays. As in the previous example, there is an ironic sting
in the tail. Voltaire's style takes on an emphatic, urgent tone:

> Forbidden on that day are both work and pleasure, a severity double
> that of the Catholic dispensation; no opera, no comedies, no concerts
> in London on Sunday; playing cards is so expressly forbidden that
> only the upper classes and the gentlemen gamble on that day. The
> rest of the nation goes to sermons, inns, or houses of ill repute.
> (Letter 6, p. 19)

Just as we are ready to pity a nation reduced to austerity and bore-
dom, banned from even playing cards, Voltaire mischievously tells us
that the nation resorts to other pleasures.

However, we are running the risk of ignoring Voltaire's observation in the twenty-second letter, that all commentators on *bons mots*
are fools. Voltaire's *Philosophical Letters* offer significantly more than
a souvenir of his time in England and a stylistic rehearsal for his subsequent stories; they also represent an early substantive statement of
abiding beliefs and ideals.

It is true that once he had left, Voltaire was never to return to
England. His sudden departure and subsequent reluctance to go
back lent some substance to rumors that he left the British Isles
under a cloud, having apparently forged banknotes. Moreover, as
wars between England and France later increased in scope and inten-
sity (reaching a pitch in the Seven Years War from 1756 to 1763 and
contested in Quebec and India as well as in Europe), it not only
became more difficult to travel, but Voltaire could also begin to
admire the momentum philosophy had achieved in France, where
Diderot and d'Alembert were working on their monumental
Encyclopédie.[4] By the time Voltaire writes and publishes his
Dictionnaire philosophique in the 1760s, he no longer arranges ideas
according to the person to whom they are attributed, as in the
Philosophical Letters, but under their own headings. Voltaire, at least
structurally, achieves a greater degree of abstraction. He is no longer
just talking about philosophers or philosophy, but being—or trying
to be—a philosopher himself.

Nonetheless, Voltaire would never tire of London nor of life. This sojurn in England left a lasting legacy and, if he would not go to England, it would increasingly come to him.[5] Likewise, although Voltaire restlessly revises texts he has written earlier, he rarely repudiates them. Indeed, even when Voltaire threw the manuscript of his epic poem, the *Henriade*, into the fire, he was careful to do so within sight of a friend, Jean Charles-Hénault, who obligingly fetched it out. In later life, Voltaire neither discards nor regrets the opinions articulated in the *Philosophical Letters*. The values and ideals that animate these pages, the vision of man, and not just the Englishman, will remain fundamental to Voltaire, subject only to minor qualifications.

It is typical of Voltaire that his view of man, and the creative and expansive philosophical discussion of which it is a part, is sparked and animated by opposition to someone Voltaire confidently believed to be totally misguided—Pascal. As usual, satirical thrusts and philosophical argument intersect in Voltaire's works. Pascal had made himself an "enemy of human nature" (Letter 25, p. 101), as Voltaire put it, by depicting humans as fragile and loathsome figures, prone to error and illusion, lost without God's guidance. Voltaire is offended by Pascal's dark portentousness, his austere condemnation of the activities that constitute an ordinary human life.[6] In opposing Pascal, Voltaire makes clear his own commitment to a contrasting view of man. Pascal sees in the relentless activities of man, the wars he wages and the pleasures he seeks, a fundamental *malaise*, a need to distract ourselves from the thoughts of our own misery and mortality. Pascal regrets man's incapacity to remain at rest, contemplating the true state of things.

In his *Pensées*, Pascal writes a beautiful, moving passage about the evanescence of the present and our inability to think about it, let alone live meaningfully in it. Voltaire quotes, "We scarcely think of the present; and if we do think about it, it is only to gain some insight so that we can plan the future" (Letter 25, p. 111). Voltaire does not contradict Pascal's view. He merely wishes to contest Pascal's supposition that this is a regrettable, tragic outcome. Unwilling to appreciate the sad lyricism of Pascal's words, Voltaire responds that:

> If men were so unfortunate as to think only of the present, no one would sow grain, nor build, nor plant, nor provide for anything: all would lack for everything in the midst of this illusory enjoyment. (Letter 25, p. 111)

In later years, Voltaire would lead a life on his own estate where, as though vindicating the insight here, he himself sows, builds, and plants. Voltaire is convinced that man is born for action. This propensity not only saves us from gloomy introspection but is responsible for improving man's condition. Action results in empirical insights. Contemplation, even a concentrated burst of reason, would not have come up with inoculation. It took the action of a falling apple and the act of looking at it to stimulate the understanding of gravitation.

Perhaps Voltaire's optimism and energy rest on a perception of man that is in its own way nevertheless bleak. Man has nothing to see or marvel at within himself. Voltairean man is empty.[7] Voltaire projects a vision of man and society that is on occasion worldly, without illusion, and even sometimes cynical. But if the fact that money and self-interest seem to govern human affairs is regrettable, Voltaire shows that these motives can be instrumental in constructing a society that is fair and coherent, while the religious ideals that would buttress this society lend themselves all too easily to abuse. As cynical as he might be now and then, Voltaire can also be enthusiastic, idealistic, and even impressionable in depicting a commercial society that is essentially benign.

In surveying intellectual history and its haphazard course in England and Europe, Voltaire observes that progress has often been guaranteed by individuals fortunate to find themselves in the right time, attuned to the needs or tastes of that particular era. As a playwright who was used to gauging his audiences—and, indeed, an actor accustomed to looking at and playing to them—Voltaire spoke powerfully and persuasively to his contemporaries, and never more so than in the *Philosophical Letters*. But in adapting himself so successfully to his own age and its needs, Voltaire risked appealing less to the ages that followed it. His various triumphs and the approval he earned from his contemporaries may have cost him some respect in later eras. This, broadly, is the argument proffered by Roland Barthes in his excellent, if slightly resentful, essay entitled "Voltaire, the Last Happy Writer."[8]

In the twelfth letter, Voltaire grants that Francis Bacon's *Novum Scientarium* was the scaffold with which philosophy was built and recognizes that scaffolds serve an important, albeit temporary, purpose. Just as Bacon's arguments and entreaties have been pushed aside by subsequent texts, so many of the debates that excited and enraged Voltaire by turns, from inoculation to gravitation, have of course long since ceased. What remains is the intelligence, courage, and charm with which Voltaire builds his arguments, which themselves remain exemplary and inspiring. Although no one, it seems, ever replied to Voltaire's *Philosophical Letters*, the fact that his correspondence travels only in one direction allows us all the more, in reading these letters, to continue supplying our own responses and, in so doing, to bring them to renewed life.

John Leigh

Translator's Note

Voltaire's prose is clear and classical; there are few eighteenth-century idioms that pose difficulties for readers or translators. I have tried to make this translation as clear as the original. When I have had a choice of words, I have tried to use those whose meaning is substantially the same in eighteenth-century and in modern English. Occasionally I have allowed word order to reflect the eighteenth-century idiom, simply to remind readers that the text is set in a particular time. I have had the benefit of consulting the first English translation of the *Philosophical Letters*, which appeared in London in 1733, shortly before the first French edition appeared.[1] In addition, I have been able to use Henry Pemberton's *A View of Sir Isaac Newton's Philosophy* (London, 1728),[2] which Voltaire himself used in writing the chapters on Newton.

The French text is the one published by Gallimard, with notes prepared by Frederic Deloffre (1986).[3] It is the text published originally by Jore in 1734; this edition and later ones included the final letter (Letter 25, on Pascal), which did not appear in the 1733 English edition.

I would like to thank William Stoneman, Director of the Houghton Library at Harvard University, who made the 1733 English translation available to me; Owen Gingrich, Professor Emeritus of Astronomy and History of Science at Harvard University, who let me borrow Isaac Pemberton's work on Newton; and Jack Iverson, whose careful reading was indispensable. Finally, I thank my parents, Harold F. and Bertha R. Linder, who provided me with my first introduction to the French language.

Prudence L. Steiner

FIRST LETTER

On the Quakers

It seemed to me that the doctrine and the history of so extraordinary a group deserved investigation by some thoughtful person. To learn about them, I sought out one of the most famous Quakers in England, who, after thirty years in trade, knew how to set limits on his fortune and his desires, and had withdrawn to the countryside near London.[1] I went to find him in his retreat; it was a small, well-built house, clean and without decorations. The Quaker was a fresh-looking old man who had never been ill because he had never known either passion or intemperance: I have never in my life seen a more noble or a more engaging countenance than his. He was dressed like all others of his religion, in a coat unpleated at the sides, and without buttons on the pockets or sleeves; and he carried a large flat-brimmed hat like those of our clergymen. He received me with his hat on his head, and came toward me without the slightest bow, but there was more politeness in his open and humane appearance than there is in someone who has the custom of pulling one leg behind the other and carrying in his hand what should be on his head.[2]

"Friend," said he, "I see that thou art a foreigner; if I can be of use to thee, thou hast only to ask."[3]

"Sir," said I, bowing and making a leg as is our custom, "I flatter myself that my honest curiosity will not displease you, and that you would be kind enough to do me the honor of instructing me about your religion."

"The people of thy country," he replied, "use too many compliments and bows; but I have not yet seen one who had the same curiosity that thou hast. Come in, and let us first dine together."

I offered a few more lame compliments, because one does not change one's customs all at once; and after a healthy and frugal meal, which began and ended with a prayer to God, I set about to question my man. I began with the question that good Catholics frequently ask Huguenots:[4]

"Dear Sir," said I to him, "have you been baptized?"

"No," answered the Quaker, "and neither are my brethren." "What the deuce!" I replied, "then are you not Christians?"

1

"My son," he replied gently, "do not swear. We are indeed Christians, and we try to be good Christians, but we do not believe that Christianity depends on throwing cold water and a bit of salt on the head."

"Zounds!" I answered, "apart from this heresy, have you then forgotten that Jesus Christ was baptized by John?"

"Friend, please do not swear again," said the benevolent Quaker. "Christ received baptism from John, but he never baptized anyone; we are not John's disciples but Christ's."

"Alas," said I, "how quickly you would be burned in a country with an Inquisition, my poor fellow! . . . For the love of God, let me baptize you and make a Christian of you!"

"If that were enough to reassure thee we would gladly be baptized," he replied gravely. "We do not condemn anyone for using the ceremony of baptism, but we believe that those who profess a holy and spiritual religion should abstain as much as possible from Jewish ceremonies."

"Yet another!" I cried. "Jewish ceremonies!"

"Yes, my son," he continued, "and so Jewish that even today many Hebrews practice the baptism of John. Look at history: It will teach thee that John simply restored this practice, which long before his day had been the custom among the Jews, as was a pilgrimage to Mecca among the Ishmaelites. Jesus was quite willing to receive baptism from John, just as he submitted to circumcision; but circumcision and ritual washing were both abolished by the baptism of Christ, this baptism of the spirit, this baptism that cleanses the soul and that saves mankind. Thus said His precursor, John: 'I indeed baptize you with water, but one will come after me, more powerful than I, whose sandals I am not worthy to bear; this one will baptize you by fire and the Holy Spirit.' And the great apostle to the Gentiles, Paul, wrote to the Corinthians, 'Christ did not send me to baptize ye, but to preach the Gospel.' And indeed this same Paul baptized with water only two persons—and that despite himself; he did circumcise his disciple Timothy; the other apostles circumcised those who wished it.—Art thou circumcised?" he added. I told him that I had not had the honor. "Well, then," said he, "my friend, thou art a Christian without being circumcised, and I without being baptized."

Thus did my saintly man speciously distort three or four passages of Holy Writ that seemed to support his sect;[5] while he, in good faith, was forgetting a hundred that would have crushed him. I carefully refrained from challenging him: nothing is gained by confronting an enthusiast: it is not prudent to point out the defects of his mistress to a lover, or the weakness of his arguments to a plaintiff, nor his illogic to a fanatic.

"With respect to communion," I asked, "what do you do?" "We do not celebrate this." "What! No communion?" "None, except for the communion of hearts." And again he cited Scripture. He preached a fine sermon against communion, and spoke in inspired tones to prove that the sacraments were simply human inventions, and that the word *sacrament* appears nowhere in the Gospels.

"Forgive my ignorance," said he, "I have not told thee one hundredth of all the justifications for our religion, but thou canst find them in Robert Barclay's treatise on our faith; it is one of the best books ever written by man. Our enemies acknowledge that it is very dangerous; this proves how reasonable it is." I promised to read this book, and my Quaker believed me converted already.[6]

Then he explained briefly the strange customs that expose this sect to the scorn of others. "Admit," said he, "that thou hadst some difficulty preventing thyself from laughing when I replied to thy civilities with my hat on my head and saying 'thou' to thee. Yet thou seemest too learned to be unaware that in the time of Christ none were foolish enough to substitute the plural for the singular. They said to Caesar Augustus, 'I love thee, I pray thee, I thank thee.' And he would not allow people to call him Master, *Dominus*.[7] It was only long after his day that men chose to call each other *you* instead of *thou*, as if each one were doubled, and to usurp the titles of Majesty, Eminence, Holiness, with which worms address other worms, assuring them that they are, with utmost respect and shocking insincerity, their most humble and obedient servants. It is to protect us against using lies and flattery that we say 'thee' to kings and shoemakers; that we do not bow to anyone, and have for each man only charity, and respect only for the law.

"We dress somewhat differently from other men, so that we are always warned not to resemble them. Others wear their badges of honor; we wear our Christian humility; we flee idle pleasure, theaters, games; we would be much pitied if these trifles filled the hearts in which God dwells; we never take an oath, not even in a court of law; we believe that the name of the Almighty should not be prostituted in a miserable human controversy. When we must appear before magistrates for some business that involves others (for we never ourselves go to law) we affirm the truth by a *yes* or a *no* and the judges believe what we have said while so many Christians perjure themselves on the Bible. We do not go to war; it is not because we fear death—on the contrary, we bless the moment that unites us with the Supreme Being—but because we are neither wolves, nor tigers, nor hounds, but men, but Christians. Our God, who commanded us to love our enemies and to suffer without complaint, surely does not want us to cross the sea to cut our brothers' throats simply because murderers in red coats, wearing hats two feet tall, enlist citizens by thumping on a drum; and after battles are won, when all of London is illuminated, the sky is full of fireworks, the air resounds with thanksgivings, with bells, with organs, with cannons, we groan in silence for the murders that have caused this public jubilation."

SECOND LETTER

On the Quakers

Such was, more or less, the conversation that I had with this curious man; but I was much more surprised when, the next Sunday, he took me to the Quakers' church. They have many chapels in London; the one to which I went is near the famous pillar called *The Monument*.[1] They had already gathered when I entered with my guide. There were about four hundred men in the church and three hundred women: the women hid their faces behind their fans; the men wore their large hats; all were seated in profound silence. I walked between them without one of them lifting his eyes to me. This silence lasted a quarter of an hour. Finally one of the men rose, took off his hat, and after a few grimaces and sighs, began braying—partly through his mouth, partly through his nose—a jumble drawn from the Gospels, or so he thought, which neither he nor anyone else understood. Once this contortionist had finished his fine monologue, and the meeting had gone its way, edified and still ignorant, I asked my man why the wise among them put up with such foolishness. "We are obliged to tolerate it," said he, "because we cannot know whether a man who rises to speak will be inspired by the Spirit or by folly; being in doubt, we listen quite patiently; indeed, we even allow women to speak. A few of our most pious women find themselves inspired at the same moment; and then there is a joyful noise in the Lord's house."— "Then you have no priests?" said I. —"No, my friend," said the Quaker, "and we are quite happy so. God forbid that we dare choose one person to receive the Holy Spirit on Sunday, and not others. Thank Heaven that we are the only ones on earth who have no priests. Wouldst thou take from us so happy a distinction? Why would we abandon our child to a hired wet nurse, when we ourselves have milk to give it? These hirelings would soon become masters in the house, oppressing mother and child. God has said, 'Freely have ye received; freely give.' Should we, after this teaching, set about to trade in the Gospel, sell the Holy Spirit, and turn a Christian congregation into a tradesman's shop? We do not give money to black-clad men to help our poor, to bury our dead, to preach to the faithful; these holy offices are too dear to us for us to hand them over to others."

5

"But how can you tell," I pressed him, "whether it is the Spirit of God that inspires your discourse?" Said he, "Whoever prays to God to enlighten him, and who preaches the Gospel truths that he feels within him, can assure himself that God has inspired him." Then he overwhelmed me with quotations from Scripture that proved, he said, that there can be no Christianity without direct revelation, and he added these extraordinary words: "When thou movest one of thy limbs, is it thine own strength that moves it? No, surely not, for this limb often moves involuntarily. It is thus the one who created thy body who moves this earthly body. And the ideas in thy soul; is it thou who formest them? Still less, for they come despite thyself. It is thus the creator of thy soul who gives thee thy ideas; but as he has left thy heart its freedom, he gives thy spirit the ideas that thy heart deserves. Thou livest in God; thou actest, thinkest in God; thou hast but to open thy eyes to this light that shines on all men; then thou wilt see the truth and make it known." "Eh! Here is Father Malebranche to the letter!"[2] I cried.—"I know thy Malebranche," said he. "He was something of a Quaker, but not quite enough."

These are the most important things that I learned concerning the Quaker doctrine. In the next letter you will have their history, which you will find even more remarkable than their doctrine.

Third Letter

On the Quakers

You have already seen that the Quakers date back to Jesus Christ, who was, they say, the first Quaker. Religion, say they, was corrupted almost immediately after his death, and continued in that corrupt form for about sixteen hundred years; but there were always a few Quakers hidden here and there who carefully guarded the sacred flame—extinguished everywhere else—until at last its light spread out in England in the year 1642.

During the years when three or four religious sects were tearing Great Britain apart in civil wars started in the name of God, a certain George Fox of Leicestershire, son of a silk worker, took it into his head to preach as a true apostle, which is to say knowing neither how to read nor write; he was a youth of twenty-five, of irreproachable conduct and saintly folly.[1] He was clothed in leather from head to foot; he went from village to village denouncing war and the clergy. Had he only preached against the army, he would have had nothing to fear, but he also attacked the Church; he was soon put in prison. He was led to the justice of the peace in Derby. Fox appeared before the justice with his leather hat on his head. A sergeant at arms gave him a great buffet, saying, "Wretch, do you not know you must bare your head before His Honor the judge?" Fox turned the other cheek and besought the sergeant to kindly give him another such buffet for the love of God. The Derby justice of the peace wanted him to swear an oath before interrogating him. "My friend, thou must be assured that I never take the name of God in vain." The justice, seeing that this man called him "thou," sent him to the Derby Madhouse to be whipped. George Fox went forth, praising God all the way to the madhouse, where they did not fail to execute the sentence rigorously. Those who whipped him were most surprised when he begged them to give him a few more lashes for the good of his soul. Those gentlemen did not need to be asked; Fox had a double dose, for which he thanked them most cordially. He began to preach to them; at first they laughed; then they listened; and, since enthusiasm is a contagious disease, many were persuaded, and those who had whipped him became his first disciples.

7

Released from prison, he ran about the countryside with a dozen converts, always preaching against the clergy and sometimes being whipped. One day he held forth from the pillory with such force that some fifty of his hearers were converted, and the rest so took his part that he was tumultuously pulled out of the stocks; the Anglican clergyman whose authority had condemned Fox to this ordeal was fetched and pilloried in his stead.

He dared to convert some of Cromwell's soldiers, who abandoned their military profession and refused to take the oath.[2] Cromwell would have nothing to do with a sect that forbade fighting, just like Pope Sixtus the Fifth, who condemned a religious order 'dove non si chiavava.'[3] He used his power to persecute these newcomers; the prisons were filled with them, but persecutions almost always serve only to make proselytes; they came out of prisons strengthened in their beliefs, and followed by the jailors whom they had converted. Now what most enabled the sect to grow was this: Fox believed himself inspired. He thought, therefore, that he must speak differently from others; he began to tremble, to grimace and twist himself about, to hold his breath or to pant violently; the Delphic oracles could have done no better. He quickly acquired the habit of inspired speech, and it soon became impossible for him to speak otherwise. This was the first of the gifts he imparted to his disciples. They copied the grimaces of their master in good faith; they trembled with all their might at the moment of inspiration. And thus they acquired the name "Quakers," or those who tremble. Lesser folk took pleasure in imitating them. They trembled; they spoke through their noses; they had convulsions; they thought themselves possessed by the Holy Ghost. They needed some miracles, and wrought them.

Fox the patriarch publicly announced to a justice of the peace, in the presence of a large gathering, "Friend, take care; God will soon punish thee for persecuting the saints." This judge was a drunkard who daily drank too much bad beer and spirits; he died of apoplexy two days later, just after he had signed an order to commit several Quakers to prison. This sudden death was not attributed to his intemperance; everyone believed it was the result of the holy man's prediction.

This death created more Quakers than a thousand sermons and as many convulsions could have done. Cromwell, seeing their numbers grow every day, wished to enlist them in his cause; he offered them money, but they were incorruptible; and he said one day that their religion was the only one that he failed to persuade with gold.

They were sometimes persecuted under Charles II, not for their religion, but for refusing to pay their tithe to the clergy, for saying "thou" to magistrates, and for refusing to take the oaths required by law.[4]

At last, in 1675, the Scotsman Robert Barclay presented to the king his *Apology for the Quakers*, a work as good as it could possibly be.[5] The dedication to Charles II contains not base flattery but daring truths and wise counsel.

"Thou hast tasted," said he to Charles at the end of the dedication, "the sweet and the bitter, prosperity and the greatest of misfortunes; thou hast been chased from the country where thou reignest; thou hast known the weight of oppression, and thou shouldst know how detestable is the oppressor in the eyes of God and of man. If then, after such trials and blessings, thy heart was hardened and it forgot the God who remembered thee in thy disgrace, thy crime would be the greater and thy punishment the more terrible. Rather than listening to the flatterers in thy court, listen to the voice of thy conscience, which will never flatter thee. I am thy faithful friend and subject, Barclay."

What is most astonishing is that this letter, written by an obscure individual, had its effect, and the persecutions ceased.

Fourth Letter

On the Quakers

At about this time William Penn appeared, the illustrious man who established the power of the Quakers in America, and who would have made them respectable in Europe if men were able to recognize virtue beneath a foolish appearance; he was the only son of his father, a knight and vice admiral of England who was the confidant of the Duke of York, later James II.[1]

At the age of fifteen, William Penn met a Quaker at Oxford, where he was studying; this Quaker converted him, and the young man, who was lively, naturally eloquent, noble in appearance and manners, soon won over some of his comrades. He gradually formed a society of young Quakers who met at his house; and by the age of sixteen, he found himself at the head of a sect.

On his return home from college, rather than kneeling before his father the vice admiral to request his blessing, as was the custom among the English, he came before him with his hat upon his head, saying, "I am happy, dear friend, to find thee in good health." The vice admiral thought he had gone mad; he learned soon enough that he had become a Quaker. He tried by all the means that human prudence could suggest to persuade him to live as others did; the young man's response was simply to exhort his father to become a Quaker himself.

At length the father relented, asking him only to go to see the king and the Duke of York with his hat under his arm and to forbear from addressing them as "Thou." William replied that his conscience would not permit him to do so, and his father, indignant and in despair, drove him from the house. Young Penn thanked God for allowing him so soon to suffer for His cause; he went to preach in the City [of London], where he made many converts.

The sermons of the ordained ministers attracted fewer listeners every day; and since Penn was young, handsome, and attractive, the ladies of the Court and the Town rushed devoutly to hear him. His reputation drew the patriarch George Fox to London from the depths of the country; together they resolved to undertake missions to foreign countries. They set sail for Holland, having left a good

11

number of workers to tend the vineyard in London. They had much success in Amsterdam; but what honored them most, and most threatened their humility, was the reception they received from Elizabeth the Princess Palatine, aunt of George I, King of England, a woman remarkable for her intelligence and knowledge, and to whom Descartes had addressed his philosophical romance.[2]

She had retired to The Hague, where she saw these Friends, for thus were the Quakers called in Holland; she had several conversations with them, they preached frequently in her residence, and, if they did not make her into a perfect Quakeress, they did at least acknowledge that she was not far from the kingdom of Heaven.

The Friends sowed the seed in Germany also, but they harvested little. People did not fancy the custom of saying "thou" and "thee" in a country where one must always have "Highness" and "Excellency" at the tip of one's tongue. Penn soon returned to England, learning of his father's illness, and arrived to find him on his deathbed. The vice admiral was reconciled with his son and embraced him tenderly, although he was of a different religion; William urged in vain that he not receive the sacraments but die a Quaker; and the good old man unsuccessfully urged William to wear buttons on his sleeves and ribbons on his hat.

William inherited a goodly estate, including royal debts for loans made by the vice admiral to support maritime expeditions. Nothing was less secure than a debt incurred by the king; Penn had to say "thou" and "thee" to Charles II and his ministers more than once in order to be paid. In 1680, the government gave Penn, in lieu of money, governance of a province in America to the south [sic] of Maryland: here was a Quaker become a prince. He left for his new estates, with two ships full of Quakers following him; from then on the territory was called *Pennsylvania*, in his honor. There he established the city of Philadelphia, which today is flourishing. He began by making a treaty with his neighbors the [native] Americans. It is the only treaty between these people and the Christians that has never been confirmed by oath and never broken. The new ruler was also the legislator for Pennsylvania: he made wise laws, none of which has been changed since that time. The first was to prohibit maltreatment of anyone because of his religion, and to consider as brothers all those who believe in God.

Scarcely had he established his government when many American merchants came to settle in the colony. The indigenous people, rather than fleeing into the forest, gradually became accustomed to the peaceful Quakers: whereas they detested other Christians' conquest and destruction, they felt warmly toward these newcomers. In little time large numbers of the so-called savages, charmed by the gentleness of these neighbors, came in a great gathering to beg William Penn to consider them his subjects. This was a novel spectacle: a sovereign who called others "thou" and "thee," to whom one could speak with his hat on his head, a government without priests, a people without weapons, citizens all equal before the law, and neighbors devoid of envy.

William Penn might well have boasted that he brought back the golden age of which so much is spoken and which in fact never really existed save in Pennsylvania. He returned to England to attend to the affairs of his new country. After the death of Charles II, King James, who had loved his father, loved William Penn as well, and saw him no longer as an eccentric sectarian but as a truly great man. The king's policy and his affection were linked; he wished to please the Quakers by abolishing the laws against nonconformists so that he could introduce the Catholic religion under the protection of this new freedom. All the sects in England saw the trap and were not caught by it; they were all united against their common enemy, the Catholics; but Penn did not believe he had to abandon his principles to help the Protestants who hated him at the expense of a king who loved him. He had established freedom of conscience in America; he did not want to appear to destroy this freedom in Europe; thus he remained faithful to James II, even though he was generally accused of being a Jesuit. This calumny deeply pained him: he felt obliged to justify himself by published statements. Meanwhile, the unfortunate James II, who like almost all the Stuarts was a combination of greatness and weakness, and who, like the others, did both too much and too little, lost his kingdom, although no one could say how such a thing occurred.[3]

All the English sects accepted the same liberty from William III and his Parliament that they had not wanted to take from the hands of James. It was then that the Quakers began legally to enjoy all those privileges that are still theirs today. Penn, having at last seen his sect well established in the country of his birth, returned to Pennsylvania. With tears of joy, his own people and the [native] Americans received him as a father who had returned to his children. All his laws had been religiously obeyed in his absence, something that no legislator before him had ever seen. He lived for several years in Philadelphia. He left reluctantly to solicit in London new commercial opportunities to benefit Pennsylvania; he lived on in London into his very old age, seen always as the leader of a people and a religion. He died at last in 1718.

His descendants inherited the property and the governance of Pennsylvania, and they ceded the government to the crown for twelve thousand pieces.[4] The king could afford to pay only one thousand. A French reader will imagine that the king's ministers paid the rest in promises and seized the government: not at all. Since the Crown was unable to pay the remainder within the specified time, the contract was considered null and void, and the Penn family regained its rights.[5]

I cannot foretell the fate of the Quaker religion in America, but I see it dwindling daily in London. In every country the dominant religion, if it does not persecute others, eventually swallows them up. The Quakers cannot be members of Parliament or hold public office; to do so they would have to swear an oath, which they refuse to do. They are reduced to earning money by commerce. Their children, made wealthy by the industry of their fathers, now want to live in comfort, have titles, wear buttons and lace wristbands; they are ashamed of being called Quakers, and, to be fashionable, they have joined the Church of England.

FIFTH LETTER

On the Anglican Religion

This is the country of sects. An Englishman, being a free man, goes to Heaven by whatever path he chooses.

However, although each one here may serve God as he wishes, the real religion, the one by which one makes one's fortune, is the Episcopal sect called the Anglican Church, or simply the Church. One can hold no post, either in England or in Ireland, unless one is a faithful Anglican; this fact, which provides convincing proof, has converted so many nonconformists that today not more than a twentieth part of the population remains outside the dominant Church.

The Anglican clergy has retained many of the Catholic ceremonies, especially that of receiving tithes in a meticulous fashion. They also piously intend to dominate.

In addition, they encourage in their flocks as best they can a holy zeal against the nonconformists. This zeal was quite strong in the Tory government of the last years of Queen Anne's reign, but it did not go much farther than occasionally breaking some windows in the heretical chapels: for in England, sectarian passion ended with the civil wars, and the disturbances in the reign of Queen Anne were only the muffled rumblings of the sea still troubled after the tempest had subsided.[1] When the Whigs and the Tories tore at the country, like the earlier Guelphs and Ghibellines, religion necessarily became a party matter.[2] The Tories were for the episcopacy; the Whigs wished to abolish it, but were content simply to diminish it once they were in power.

When Lord Harley of Oxford and Milord Bolingbroke made the Tories the toast of the nation, the Anglican Church considered them defenders of its holy privileges.[3] The Convocation of the lower orders, a kind of ecclesiastical House of Commons, had some power then; it rejoiced in the freedom to assemble, to debate controversies, and, from time to time, to burn a few heretical books, that is, books that attacked it. The Ministry, which is now Whig, does not even permit these gentlemen to assemble; they are reduced, in the obscurity of their parishes, to the dismal obligation of praying to God for the well-being of the government that they would be pleased to disturb. As for the bishops, of which there are twenty-six, they sit in the House of Lords despite the Whigs, because the old folly of considering them barons persists;[4] but they have no more power in the House than have dukes and peers in the Parliament in Paris. There is a clause in the oath of loyalty that one swears to the state that much tries the Christian patience of these gentlemen.

That oath requires one to belong to the Church as it has been established by the law. There is scarcely a bishop, a dean, an archdeacon, who does not believe that he has been appointed by divine right; it is thus very mortifying to be obliged to admit that they hold their positions by virtue of a miserable law made by a profane laity. One cleric (Father Courayer), recently wrote a book to assert the validity and the propriety of Anglican ordination.[5] This work was proscribed in France; but do you think it was welcomed by the Anglican ministry? Not at all. Those damnable Whigs care little that the apostolic succession of bishops had been interrupted, or whether bishop Parker was ordained in a tavern (as some would have it) or in a church;[6] they prefer that the bishops hold their authority from Parliament rather than from the apostles. Lord B*** said that the idea of apostolic succession would only serve to install tyrants clad in cassock and surplice, whereas human law created citizens.[7]

As far as morals are concerned, the Anglican clergy are better behaved than are the French. Here is the reason: All churchmen are educated in the Universities of Oxford or of Cambridge, far from the corruption of the capital; they are called to the honors of the Church only after many years, at the age when men's chief passion is avarice, and their ambition has nothing to feed upon. High position in the Church, as in the army, is the reward for long service; here one does not see young bishops or colonels who have just left college. Moreover, almost all the clergy are married; the awkwardness he has acquired at the University, and his scant commerce with women, mean that a bishop is ordinarily forced to be content with his wife. Clergymen may from time to time go to taverns, since custom permits it, but if they become drunk, it is soberly and without scandal.

That indefinable being who is neither ordained nor a layman, whom we call an *abbé*, is a species of cleric unknown in England; churchmen here are all reserved in manner and almost all of them are pedants.[8] When they learn that in France young men, known for their debauchery and elevated to the prelacy by women's intrigues, flirt openly with women, amuse themselves by writing love songs, daily play the host at long and intimate suppers, and thence go off to be enlightened by the Holy Spirit, brazenly claiming to be the successors to the apostles, the English thank God that they are Protestants. But of course they are vile heretics, fit to be burnt by all the devils, as Master François Rabelais said; and I shall not involve myself with such matters.[9]

SIXTH LETTER

On the Presbyterians

Only in England and Ireland is the Anglican religion established. Presbyterianism is the dominant religion in Scotland. This Presbyterianism is simply pure Calvinism as it used to exist in France and continues in Geneva.[1] Since the priests of this sect receive but scant wages from their churches, and since, therefore, they cannot live in the luxury enjoyed by the bishops, they have naturally undertaken to preach against the honors that they cannot attain. Imagine proud Diogenes who trampled on the pride of Plato; the Scottish Presbyterians somewhat resemble that arrogant, disputatious beggar.[2] They treated King Charles II with much less respect than Diogenes offered Alexander. For, when they took up arms to support the king against Cromwell, who had betrayed them, they forced that poor king to sit through four sermons a day; they forbade him to gamble; they insisted he do penance, until Charles grew tired of being the king of such pedants and slipped from their hands as a schoolboy runs from school.

Compared to a lively young French clerk, squawking in his seminary in the morning and in the evening singing with the ladies, an Anglican priest seems a Cato;[3] and this Cato seems like a courtier compared with a Scottish Presbyterian. The latter adopts a grave demeanor, an air of disapproval, wears a great hat, a long coat over a short jacket, preaches through his nose, and calls "whores of Babylon" those churches in which some clergy are fortunate enough to earn fifty thousand pounds,[4] and whose congregations are kind enough to permit this and to call their ministers My Lord, Your Highness, Your Eminence.

These gentlemen, who have some churches in England, have made their dour and serious expressions the fashion in Scotland. It is thanks to them that Sunday has become sanctified in all three kingdoms;[5] forbidden on that day are both work and pleasure, a severity double that of the Catholic dispensation; no opera, no comedies, no concerts in London on Sunday; playing cards is so expressly forbidden that only the upper classes and the gentlemen gamble on that day. The rest of the nation goes to sermons, inns, or houses of ill repute.

19

Although the Episcopal and the Presbyterian churches are dominant in Great Britain, all sects are welcome there and all live together comfortably enough, while their preachers detest one another with almost as much cordiality as a Jansenist curses a Jesuit.

Go into the Royal Exchange in London, a building more respectable than most courts; there you will find deputies from every nation assembled simply to serve mankind.[6] There, the Jew, the Mohammedan, and the Christian negotiate with one another as if they were all of the same religion, and the only heretics are those who declare bankruptcy; there the Presbyterian trusts the Anabaptist, the Anglican accepts the word of the Quaker. Leaving this peaceful and liberal assembly, some go to the synagogue, others go to drink; this one is baptized in a great font in the name of the Father, the Son, and the Holy Spirit; that one has his son circumcised while some Hebrew words that he does not understand are mumbled over him; still others go to their church with their hats on their heads to await the inspiration of God, and all are content.

Were there only one religion in England, despotism would be a threat; were there two, they would be at each other's throats; but there are thirty, and they live happily and at peace with one another.

SEVENTH LETTER

On the Socinians, or Arians, or Antitrinitarians

There is here a small sect of very learned ecclesiastics and laymen, who do not call themselves Arian or Socinian, but who do not share the opinion of Saint Athanasius on the question of the Trinity, and who will tell you bluntly that the Father is greater than the Son.[1]

Do you remember a certain orthodox bishop who, to convince an emperor about consubstantiation, decided to take the emperor's son by the chin and pull his nose in the presence of the emperor himself? The emperor was about to become angry with the bishop, when that good man spoke these beautiful and convincing words: "My lord, if Your Majesty is angry because of the lack of respect for his son, how do you imagine that God the Father will treat those who refuse to give Jesus Christ the titles that are due Him?" The people of whom I am speaking say that this holy bishop was most imprudent, that his argument was somewhat less than conclusive, and that the emperor should have answered, "Learn that there are two ways to show me disrespect: the first is to fail adequately to honor my son; the second is to show him as much honor as you show me."[2]

However it may be, the Arians have begun to reappear in England, and also in Holland and in Poland. The great Mr. Newton honored this doctrine by agreeing with it; the philosopher believed that the Unitarians argued more mathematically than do we. But the strongest supporter of Arian doctrine is the illustrious Doctor Clarke, a man of rigid virtue and sweet temperament, a lover of his opinions rather than a proselytizer, solely engaged in calculations and proofs, a true reasoning machine.[3]

He is the author of a book, little understood but well regarded, on the existence of God, and of another, easier to understand but little valued, on the truth of the Christian religion.

He has not become engaged in handsome scholastic disputes, which our friend _____ calls venerable inanities;[4] he was content to publish a book containing all the earliest arguments for and against Unitarianism, and left the reader to follow and judge them for himself. The doctor's book attracted many supporters but prevented him from becoming the Archbishop of Canterbury; I think the doctor misjudged, and that it was better to be Primate of England than an Arian curate.

You see that revolutions occur in opinions as they do in empires. The Arian doctrine, after three hundred years of triumph and twelve centuries of neglect, was born again of its ashes; but it has returned inopportunely, at a time when the world has a surfeit of sectarian disputes. This sect is still too small to be permitted public meetings. It will obtain permission, no doubt, if it becomes larger, but everyone is so lukewarm about these matters that a new or revived religion can scarcely succeed. Is it not amusing that Luther, Calvin, Zwingli, all those unreadable writers, should have founded sects that together cover all of Europe? That ignorant Mahomet should have given a religion to Asia and Africa, and that Newton, Clarke, Locke, Le Clerc, etc., the greatest philosophers and the best writers of their time, have scarcely managed to assemble a tiny flock, one that is indeed shrinking daily?[5]

This is what it means to arrive in the world at the right moment. If Cardinal de Retz were to reappear today, he could not stir up ten women in Paris.[6]

If Cromwell were reborn, he who cut off the head of his king and made himself the sovereign, he would be a simple London merchant.[7]

EIGHTH LETTER

On the Parliament

Members of the English Parliament like to compare themselves with ancient Romans as often as they can.

Not long ago in the House of Commons Mr. Shipping[1] began his speech with these words: "The majesty of the English people would be harmed," etc. The odd nature of this expression provoked much laughter, but undismayed, he firmly repeated the same words and there was no more laughter.[2] I admit that I see no similarities between the majesty of the English people and that of the Roman people, and still less between their two governments. There is a senate in London of which some members are suspected, no doubt mistakenly, of selling their votes when convenient, as also happened in Rome: that is the only similarity. Moreover, the two nations seem entirely different to me, in virtues as in vice. The Romans never knew the dreadful folly of religious wars; this abomination was reserved for those who devoutly preach humility and patience. Marius and Sylla, Pompey and Caesar, Anthony and Augustus did not fight to decide whether the Flamen priest should wear his shirt over his robe or his robe over his shirt, and whether the sacred chickens should eat and drink or only eat to indicate the auguries. The English took turns hanging each other at the Assizes,[3] and destroyed each other in pitched battle for quarrels of this type; for a while the conflicting claims of the episcopacy and the presbytery dizzied these sober wits. I doubt that this kind of stupidity will happen again; the English seem to have gained wisdom at their own expense, and I do not see in them any further longing to cut one another's throats for the sake of a syllogism.

Here is a more significant difference between Rome and England, which shows the latter at an advantage: it is that the result of the civil wars in Rome was slavery, and in England, liberty. The English nation is the only one on earth that has managed to control the power of kings by resisting them, and which, by successive efforts, has finally established this wise government in which the prince, all-powerful for doing good, is restrained from doing harm; where the lords, who lack insolence and vassals, are yet great; and where the common people share power without disorder.

The Houses of Lords and of Commons together govern the nation; the king is above them. The Romans lacked this balance; there the powerful and the populace were always at odds, lacking a mediator who could reconcile them. The Roman Senate, whose unlawful and criminal pride forbade it to share power with the plebeians, knew no other way to distance them from government than to engage them in foreign wars. They considered the people a savage beast, to be set upon their neighbors lest it devour its masters; thus Rome's greatest defect was the very one that gave it an empire. It is because the Romans were miserable at home that they became masters of the world, until their internal divisions at last made them slaves.

The English government is designed neither for such brilliance nor for so unfortunate an end; its aim is not conquest, that dazzling folly, but to prevent its neighbors from such an endeavor; this people is jealous of its own liberty and of that of others. The English attacked Louis XIV mercilessly solely because they believed him committed to conquest. They made war lightheartedly, without self-interest.[4]

The English paid heavily to establish their liberty; the idol of despotism was drowned in seas of blood; but the English do not think they purchased their good laws at too steep a price. Other nations have not had fewer troubles, have not shed less blood than they; but the blood they have spilled in the cause of their liberty has only cemented their slavery.

What becomes a revolution in England is only a small uprising in other countries. In Spain, in Barbary, in Turkey, when a city takes up arms to defend its rights, mercenary soldiers subdue it, executioners punish it, and the rest of the country kisses its chains. The French believe that the government of this island is stormier than the sea that surrounds it, and that is true, but only when the king stirs up the tempest, when he wants to be the master of the ship rather than its pilot. Civil wars in France have been longer and more cruel, have produced more crimes than those in England; none of those wars had as its aim the establishment of well-ordered liberty.

In the detestable times of Charles IX and Henry III, the only issue was whether we would be slaves to the Guises.[5] The last war in Paris deserves only catcalls; it seems as though I am watching schoolboys who mutiny against their proctor and end up with a flogging. Cardinal de Retz, a rebel without a cause, a dissident without a plan, the head of a party that had no troops, whose wit and courage were misplaced, intrigued simply for the sake of intrigue, and seemed to provoke civil war merely to entertain himself. The French *Parlement* knew neither what he wanted nor what he did not want: he enlisted soldiers and dismissed them; he threatened; he sued for pardon; he put a price on the head of Cardinal Mazarin, and then ceremoniously came to compliment him.[6] Our civil wars in the days of Charles VI were cruel; those of the League were abominable; those of the *Fronde* were ridiculous.[7]

The French roundly condemn the English for executing Charles I, who was treated by his conquerors as he would have treated them had he won.

Yet let us compare Charles I, defeated in battle, imprisoned, judged, sentenced in Westminster, with the Emperor Henry VII, poisoned by his chaplain while taking communion; Henry III, assassinated by a monk, the envoy of his whole party's fury; thirty plots to assassinate Henri IV, many of which were attempted and the last of which deprived France of this great king.[8] Weigh these attempts and judge them.

NINTH LETTER

On the Government

In the English government, that happy conjunction, that agreement among the Commons, the Lords, and the king, did not always exist. England was for a long time enslaved to the Romans, the Saxons, the Danes, the French. William the Conqueror in particular ruled them with a scepter of iron; he seized the goods and the lives of his new subjects like an Asiatic monarch; he forbade all English, under penalty of death, to have fire and light in their dwellings after eight o'clock of the evening, perhaps because he imagined this would prevent night-time meetings, perhaps because he wanted to test, by this strange prohibition, just how far the power of one man could extend over others.[1]

It is true that before and after William the Conqueror, the English had parliaments; they boast of them as if these assemblies, named parliaments and composed of ecclesiastical tyrants and baronial robbers, were the guardians of public liberty and happiness.

The barbarians who flowed into the rest of Europe from the shores of the Baltic Sea brought with them the custom of those Estates or parliaments of which so much has been made and so little is known. The kings in those days were not despotic, to be sure; but the people only groaned all the more in their miserable slavery. The chiefs of these savages who had ravaged France, Italy, Spain, England, made themselves monarchs; their captains shared the conquered lands. Thence came those margraves, those lairds, those barons, those petty tyrants who often challenged their king for the spoils of the people. They were birds of prey vying with an eagle for the blood of the doves; each nation had a hundred tyrants rather than one master. The priests soon took sides. From earliest times the fate of the Gauls, the Germans, [and] the inhabitants of the British Isles were to be governed by their druids and the chieftains of their villages, the progenitors of barons but less tyrannical than their successors. These druids claimed to be mediators between men and their gods: they made laws; they excommunicated; they condemned to death. Little by little the Gothic and Vandal bishops succeeded them in temporal authority. The popes put themselves at their head, and with briefs, bulls, and monks, terrified kings, deposed them, had them assassinated, and drew from Europe to themselves all the money that they could grasp. The idiot Inas,[2] one of the tyrants of the English Heptarchy, was the first who, on a pilgrimage to Rome, submitted to the demand for Peter's Pence (about a crown in our currency) from each household in his territory. Soon the whole isle followed his example. England became, little by little, a province of the pope; from time to time the Holy Father sent his deputies there to extract an exorbitant tax. John Lackland finally ceded his kingdom to his Holiness, who had excommunicated him; and the barons, who received no benefit from it, drove out this miserable king. They replaced him with Louis VIII, father of Saint Louis, King of France; but they soon became disgusted with this newcomer, and sent him back across the sea.[3]

While the barons, the bishops, and the popes, all wanting to rule, ripped England apart, the commons, the most numerous and virtuous and thus the most respected group, those who had studied law and science, merchants, artisans, in short all who were not tyrants: the commons, I say, were seen by the [nobles and priests] as creatures well below the level of humanity. They could not take part in the government; they were villeins; their work, their blood, belonged to their masters, who called themselves noblemen. Most men in Europe were what they still are in the North, serfs of a lord, a kind of cattle bought and sold with the land. Centuries had to pass before justice was done to humanity, before it was thought horrible that the majority should sow and the few should harvest; and is it not fortunate for the human race that the authority of these petty brigands should have been extinguished in France by the legitimate authority of our kings, and in England by the legitimate authority of kings and the people.

Happily, the shocks to which the quarrels of kings and nobles subjected their empires more or less weakened the shackles of the nations; liberty was born in England of the quarrels of tyrants. The barons forced John Lackland and Henry III to sign the famous Charter; its chief aim was to make the kings dependent on the nobles, but it also somewhat strengthened the rest of the nation so that the people would, if necessary, support their supposed protectors. This *Magna Carta*, which is considered the sacred origin of English liberty, itself shows how little liberty was understood.[4] Its very title demonstrates that the king believed himself absolute by right, and that the barons and the clergy were able to force him to abandon this pretended right simply because they were more powerful than he.

This is how *Magna Carta* begins: "We freely grant the following privileges to the archbishops, bishops, abbots, priors, and barons of our kingdom, etc."

None of the articles of this Charter mentions the House of Commons, proof that it did not yet exist, or else existed without power. It specifies the freemen of England, sad proof that some existed who were not free. Article 32 shows that these so-called freemen owed service to their lords. Such liberty still incorporated much slavery.

In Article 21 the king orders that thenceforth his officers could seize the freemen's horses and wagons only by paying for them, a rule that appeared to the people a true confirmation of liberty because it eliminated a greater tyranny.[5]

Henry VII, that successful usurper and clever politician who pretended to love the barons but who hated and feared them, decided to push them from their lands. Thus the villeins, who little by little acquired wealth by their efforts, bought the mansions of the illustrious peers who had ruined themselves by their extravagance. Little by little all the land changed hands.

The House of Commons became stronger daily. The families of the old peerage dwindled in time; and since, properly speaking and according to law, in England only the peers are the nobility, there would be no nobles in that country if the kings had not created new barons from time to time and maintained the peerage that they so feared in earlier times, in order to provide some opposition to the Commons, which had become too powerful.

All the new peers who make up the House of Lords receive titles from the king and nothing else; almost none of them own the lands whose name they bear. One of them, the Duke of Dorset, has not an inch of land in Dorsetshire.[6]

Another is earl of a village and scarcely knows where that village is. They have power in Parliament and nowhere else.

Here you do not hear of high, middle, and low justice,[7] nor of the right to hunt on a citizen's land while denying the owner the right to fire a gun in his own fields.

Even if a man is noble or a clergyman, he is not exempt from certain taxes; all taxes are regulated by the House of Commons, which, though only the lower house in rank, is held in esteem by the upper house.

The lords and bishops may well reject a tax bill proposed by the House of Commons, but they may not change it; they must accept or reject it without qualifications. When the bill is confirmed by the lords and approved by the king, then everyone pays the tax. Each gives, not according to his status (which is absurd) but according to his revenue; there are neither *taille*[8] nor *capitation arbitraire*[9] but only a tax on land. These lands were all assessed in the reign of the famous king William III and valued well below their price.[10]

The tax rate stays the same, although the revenue from the lands increases; thus no one is crushed under the tax, and no one complains. The countryman's feet are not crushed in wooden clogs; he eats white bread; he is well clad; and he does not hesitate to increase his flocks or cover his roof with tiles lest his taxes be raised the following year. Many of these men are worth two hundred thousand francs and do not disdain working the land that has enriched them and on which they live as free men.

Tenth Letter

On Commerce

Commerce, which has enriched the citizens of England, has contributed to their freedom, and this freedom has in turn stimulated commerce; thus has the greatness of the State been magnified. Commerce has, little by little, developed the strength of the navy, which makes the English the rulers of the seas. They have at present almost two hundred warships. Posterity will perhaps be surprised to learn that a small island that had but a little lead, tin, fuller's earth, and coarse wool, became by its commerce powerful enough in 1723 to send three fleets at the same time to three separate parts of the globe, one to Gibraltar, which was conquered and occupied by English arms, another to Porto Bello to snatch from the Spanish king his enjoyment of the riches of the Indies, and the other to the Baltic to keep the Northern Powers from fighting one another.[1]

When Louis XIV made Italy tremble, and his armies, already the masters of Savoy and Piedmont, were on the verge of capturing Turin, Prince Eugene had to march to the rescue of the Duke of Savoy from the depths of Germany. He had no money, without which no one can take or defend cities; he turned to English merchants, and in a half hour, they lent him fifty millions. With this he relieved Turin, beat the French, and wrote to those who had lent him this sum a short letter: "Gentlemen, I received your money, and I flatter myself that I have used it to your satisfaction."[2]

All this is cause for justifiable pride to an English merchant and allows him to compare himself, and not without reason, to a Roman citizen. Indeed, the younger son of a peer of the realm is not disdainful of commerce. Lord Townshend, a minister of state, has a brother who is content to be a London merchant.[3] At the time when Milord Oxford governed England, his younger brother was a business agent in Aleppo, whence he did not wish to return and where he died.[4]

This custom, which, however, is beginning to fade in England, seems monstrous to the Germans who are intoxicated by their lineage. They cannot imagine that the son of a peer of England might simply be a rich and powerful townsman, when in Germany everyone is a prince: there have been as many as thirty Highnesses bearing the same name, whose only wealth is a coat of arms and pride.

In France, anyone who wants to be a marquis may be one; and whoever comes to Paris from the depths of a province with some money to spend and a name ending in *ac* or *ille*, can say, "A man like myself, a gentleman of my class," and loftily snub a merchant. The merchant so often hears himself scorned that he is foolish enough to be ashamed of it. I, however, do not know which is the more useful to the State: a nobleman in a powdered wig who knows exactly when the king arises and when he retires, and who gives himself airs of greatness while he plays the slave in the antechamber of a minister; or a merchant who enriches his country, who sends orders from his counting house to Surat and Cairo, and contributes to the well-being of the world.

ELEVENTH LETTER

On Smallpox Inoculation

In Christian Europe people whisper that the English are deranged
and demented: deranged because they give smallpox to their children
to keep them from catching it, and demented because they cheerfully expose their children to a certain and dreadful malady to prevent
their catching something they may never have.[1] On their side the
English say: "The other Europeans are cowards and unnatural parents: cowards because they fear doing some slight harm to their children, and unnatural because they expose their children to death from
smallpox one day." To decide which view is correct, let us look at the
history of this inoculation, about which those who are outside of
England speak with such fear.

From time immemorial, Circassian women have had the practice
of giving smallpox to their children, even to those who are but six
months old, by making a small incision in the arm and inserting into
this incision a blister that they have carefully removed from another child.[2] On the arm where it has been inserted this blister acts like
yeast in a bit of dough; it ferments and spreads into the blood the
qualities with which it is impregnated. The blisters of a child to
whom one has thus artificially given the smallpox can in turn be
used to give the disease to others. There is an almost universal circulation in Circassia; and when, unfortunately, there is no smallpox
in the land, the inhabitants are at as much of a loss as if there were
a famine.

What prompted the Circassians to introduce this custom, which
seems so strange to others, is a motive common to all: maternal love
and self-interest.

The Circassians are poor and their daughters are beautiful; and
these daughters become, therefore, the chief commodity of trade.
They supply the beauties for the harems of the Great Pasha,[3] the
Grand Sophi[4] of Persia, and of those wealthy enough to buy and
maintain such precious merchandise. They conscientiously and virtu-
ously teach their daughters to caress men, to dance gracefully and
seductively, to kindle by the most voluptuous artifices the desires of
the haughty masters for whom they are destined; these poor creatures

practice their lessons with their mothers every day, as our little daughters repeat their catechism, without understanding any of it.

Now, it frequently happened that a father and mother, after having been at pains to provide a good education to their children, would see their hopes suddenly destroyed: smallpox would infect a family, one daughter would die, another would lose an eye, a third would emerge from the disease with a swollen nose, and the poor family was ruined beyond repair. Often, indeed, during a smallpox epidemic, this trade was interrupted for many years, which created a noticeable dwindling of the seraglios in Persia and Turkey.

A nation of merchants is always attentive to its interests and never ignores knowledge that can be useful to its trade. The Circassians noticed that scarcely one in a thousand has twice been afflicted with smallpox; that in fact one might have a light case of smallpox three or even four times, but never a second case that could be called serious or dangerous; in short, that never would one truly have this illness twice in one's life. They noticed, too, that in mild cases of smallpox, when the pox scarcely emerge from a fine and delicate complexion, they leave no scars on the face. From these observations of nature they concluded that if a child as young as six months or a year old had a mild case of smallpox, it would not die, would not be scarred, and would be free of this malady for the rest of its life.

Thus all that had to be done to save the life and the beauty of their children was to give them smallpox at an early age; and this is what they did, inserting into the child's body a smallpox blister taken from someone who had a complete yet not harmful case of the disease.

The experiment could not fail to succeed. The Turks, wise people, adopted the custom soon afterwards, and today there is no Pasha in Constantinople who fails to give smallpox to his son and his daughter while they are being weaned.

Some argue that the Circassians took this custom from the Arabs, but we will allow some learned Benedictine to elucidate this historical fact, and he will not fail to fill several in-folio volumes with proofs.[5] All that I can say on this matter is that at the beginning of the reign of George I, one of the wittiest and most intelligent women in England, Lady Wortley-Montagu, then in Constantinople with her husband the ambassador, decided without hesitation to give smallpox to her son who was born there.[6] Although her chaplain insisted that this was not a Christian practice and could only succeed among the infidels, the lad survived splendidly. Upon her return to London, Lady Wortley told the story to the Princess of Wales, who is now the Queen. I must say that despite all her titles and crowns, this princess was born to encourage the arts and the well-being of mankind; even on the throne she is a benevolent philosopher; she has never lost an opportunity to learn or to manifest her generosity. Learning that one of Milton's daughters was still living and was living in poverty, it was the Princess of Wales who immediately sent her a large gift;[7] it was she who protected poor Father Courayer,[8] she who was willing to mediate between Doctor Clarke and M. Leibnitz. As soon as she learned about the process of inoculation for smallpox, she tested the process on four criminals who had been condemned to death, thus doubly saving their lives by this artificial means, for she not only released them from the penalty but also saved them from natural smallpox, of which they would doubtless have died at a more advanced age.

The Princess, reassured by this test, had her children inoculated.[9] All England followed her example, and since then at least ten thousand well-born lads owe their lives to the Queen and to Lady Wortley-Montagu, and as many young girls owe to them their beauty.

Of one hundred people in the world at least sixty will have smallpox; of these sixty twenty will die in the prime of life, and twenty will survive with nasty scars; thus a fifth of humanity will inevitably be killed or badly damaged by this disease. Of all those who are inoculated in Turkey or England, none dies unless he is unwell or already dying, none is scarred, and, if the inoculation is successful, none has the disease a second time. It is thus certain that if some French ambassadress had brought back this secret from Constantinople, she would have done her nation an eternal service: the Duke of Villequier, father of the present Duke of Aumont, the strongest and healthiest man in all of France, would not have died in the prime of life.

Prince Soubise, who had perfect health, would not have been carried off at the age of twenty-five; Monseigneur,[10] the grandfather of Louis XV, would not have been buried in his fiftieth year; twenty thousand who died of smallpox in Paris in 1723 would still be alive. Now, do the French not love life? Do their wives not care about their beauty? In truth, we are a strange people! Perhaps ten years from now we will adopt this English custom if the priests and the physicians permit it; or else three months from now the French will begin inoculation on a whim, if the English reject it by inconsistency.

I have learned that the Chinese have had this custom for a hundred years; it must be prejudice that rejects the example of a nation that is believed to be the wisest and the best governed in the world. It is true that the Chinese use a different method; instead of making an incision they inhale the material as if it were snuff; this more pleasant method produces the same effect, and demonstrates equally well that if inoculation had been practiced in France, it would have saved the lives of millions of men.

TWELFTH LETTER

On Chancellor Bacon

Not long ago a well-known group busied itself in debating this time-worn and frivolous question: Which was the greatest man—Caesar, Alexander, Tamerlane, Cromwell, etc.

Someone proposed that it was without doubt Isaac Newton. That man was right, for if true greatness consists in having received from Heaven a powerful intelligence and in using that intelligence to enlighten oneself and others, then a man like Mr. Newton, whom one might scarcely hope to encounter in the course of ten centuries, truly should be deemed great; and these politicians and conquerors, who can be found in any century, are no more than illustrious villains. We owe respect to him who influences the mind by the means of truth, not to those who make slaves by violence, to him who understands the Universe, not to those who disfigure it.[1]

Now, since you ask me to tell you about the famous men of England, I will begin with Bacon, Locke, and Newton. The generals and ministers will have to wait their turn.

We should begin with the famous Viscount Verulam, known in Europe as Bacon, his family name. He was a son of a Warden of the Seals, and for many years he was Lord Chancellor in the reign of James I.[2] Yet, despite court intrigues and the preoccupations of his office, which required a man's full attention, he found the time to become a great philosopher, a good historian, and an elegant writer; all this, astonishingly, in an age when scarcely anyone knew how to write well or to be a good philosopher. He was, as often happens, more esteemed after his death than during his life: his enemies were at the Court in London; his admirers were to be found throughout Europe.[3]

When the Marquis of Effiat[4] brought Princess Marie, daughter of Henry the Great,[5] to England to marry the Prince of Wales,[6] this minister went to visit Bacon, who, being ill, received him in bed with the curtains closed. "You are like the angels," said Effiat to him. "One hears of them often, believes them to be superior to human beings, and never has the satisfaction of seeing them."

You know, dear Sir, that Bacon was accused of allowing himself to be bribed, a crime that is hardly worthy of a philosopher; you know that he was condemned by the House of Lords to pay a fine of about four hundred thousand pounds of our money, and to forfeit his position of Lord Chancellor and his peerage.[7]

Today the English so revere his memory that they do not want to admit that he was guilty. If you ask what I think, I will use a witticism that I heard from my lord Bolingbroke. Someone in his presence was speaking of the avarice attributed to the Duke of Marlborough, citing the characteristics to which Lord Bolingbroke might appropriately bear witness, since he was an avowed enemy of Marlborough. "He was such a great man," said he, "that I have forgotten his vices."

I will, then, limit myself to writing about those matters that earned for Lord Bacon the esteem of all Europe.

The most remarkable and best of his works is the one that today is least read and least useful: I mean his *Novum Organum*.[8] It is the scaffolding on which the new philosophy was built, and when this new edifice was partly raised, the scaffolding was of no further use.

Chancellor Bacon did not yet understand nature, but he knew and pointed out all the paths that would lead to it. Early on he had dismissed what the universities called "philosophy," and he did all that he could to prevent these institutions, established to perfect human reason, from continuing to harm reason with their "quiddities," their "abhorrence of the void," their "substantial forms," and all those irrelevant words made respectable by ignorance and sacred by a ridiculous association with religion.

He is the father of experimental philosophy. It is quite true that before his day astonishing secrets had been discovered. The compass, printing, engraving, oil painting, mirrors, the secret of restoring the sight of old people by means of lenses called "eyeglasses," gunpowder, etc., had all been invented. The new world had been sought, found, and conquered. Who would not believe that these sublime discoveries were made by the greatest philosophers, and in ages more enlightened than our own? Not at all: It was in the age of the most stupid barbarism that these great changes appeared. Chance alone produced most of these inventions, and it even seems that what one might call chance played a great part in the discovery of America; at least, it has always been believed that Christopher Columbus undertook his great voyage only because he trusted a captain whose vessel had been driven by storm to the latitude of the Caribbean islands.

However it may have happened, men knew how to go to the ends of the earth; they knew how to destroy cities with an artificial thunder more terrible than the natural one, but they knew nothing of the circulation of the blood, the weight of air, the laws of motion, the nature of light, the number of our planets, etc., and a man who defended a thesis on Aristotelian categories, or on the universals as they exist *a parte rei*, or other such foolishness, was considered a prodigy of learning.[9]

The most astonishing and the most useful inventions are not those that do most honor to the human mind.

We owe all the arts to mechanical instinct, which most men share, and not to orthodox philosophy.

The discovery of fire, the art of baking bread, of smelting and working metals, of building houses, the construction of the weaver's shuttle, are of much greater importance than printing and the compass; yet these were invented by men who still were savages.

What prodigious use did the Greeks and Romans not make of these mechanical inventions? Yet in their days they believed that the heavens were crystalline, that the stars were little lamps that fell into the sea from time to time, and one of their great philosophers, after much research, declared that the heavenly bodies were pebbles that had been detached from the earth.

In a word, no one before Chancellor Bacon had known of experimental philosophy; and of all the experiments that have been done since his time there is scarcely one that is not mentioned in his book. He himself undertook several of them: he made various kinds of pneumatic devices by which he deduced the elasticity of air; he approached and almost attained an understanding of its weight; this discovery was made by Torricelli.[10] Shortly thereafter, experimental physical science began suddenly to be studied throughout almost all of Europe. It was a buried treasure whose existence Bacon suspected, and that all philosophers, encouraged by his assertions, exerted themselves to unearth.

Now, what surprised me most was to find in his book a clear statement of this new attractive force that Mr. Newton, it is thought, was the first to discover.

"We must examine," said Bacon, "whether there is not some magnetic force that operates between the earth and heavy objects, between the moon and the ocean, between the planets, etc."

In another place he said, "Either heavy bodies must be carried toward the center of the earth, or each attracts the other, and in the latter case it is clear that the closer the falling bodies come to the earth, the more strongly will they be attracted. We must," he continued, "test whether the same pendulum clock will go faster upon a mountain or in the depths of a mine; if the force of the pendulum diminishes on the mountain and increases in the mine, it would seem that the earth does have attractive force."

This precursor of philosophy was also an elegant writer, a historian, a witty and considerable thinker.

His essays on morality are highly esteemed, but they are written rather to instruct than to please; and being neither satires of human nature like the *Maxims* of M. de La Rochefoucauld, nor based in skepticism like the essays of Montaigne, they are less frequently read than these two ingenious works.[11]

His *History of Henry VII* is considered a masterwork, but I doubt that it can be compared to the work of our own illustrious de Thou.[12]

Writing of that famous impostor Parkins,[13] a Jew by birth who, encouraged by the Duchess of Burgundy, so boldly took the name of Richard IV, King of England, and who challenged the claim of Henry VII to the throne, here is what Chancellor Bacon said:

"At about this time King Henry was possessed by evil spirits generated by the magic of the Duchess of Burgundy, who summoned from Hades the ghost of Edward IV to torment King Henry.

"After the Duchess of Burgundy had instructed Parkins, she began to think about where in the heavens she should make this comet appear, and she decided it should first burst forth on the Irish horizon."

It seems to me that our wise de Thou does not succumb to such inflated language, which some used to consider sublime and which now is rightly called nonsense.

Thirteenth Letter

On Mr. Locke

Perhaps there never was a wiser, more methodical, more logical mind than that of Mr. Locke, and yet he was not a great mathematician.[1] He had never been able to submit to the fatigue of calculation nor to the dryness of mathematical truths, which at first produce nothing perceptible to the spirit, and no one has demonstrated better than he that one could have the spirit of a mathematician without the help of geometry. Before his time, great philosophers had announced unequivocally what constitutes the soul of man; but, since they knew nothing about it, it is understandable that all had different opinions.

In Greece, the cradle of arts and errors, where wisdom and foolishness had been so much developed, all reasoned as we do about the soul.

The great Anaxagoras,[2] to whom an altar was dedicated because he taught men that the sun was larger than the Peloponnese, that snow was black and that the heavens were made of stone, affirmed that the soul was an airy spirit and nonetheless immortal.

Diogenes, different from the one who became a cynic after having been a counterfeiter, insisted that the soul is a part of God's substance, and this idea was at the least a brilliant one.

Epicurus imagined that the soul, like the body, was composed of various parts. Aristotle, whose work has been interpreted in thousands of ways because it is unintelligible, believed, according to some of his disciples, that all human understanding is of one and the same substance.

The divine Plato, teacher of the divine Aristotle, and the divine Socrates, teacher of the divine Plato, claimed that the soul was corporeal and eternal; Socrates' daimon no doubt told him what its nature was. There are, indeed, those who believe that a man who boasted of having a familiar spirit was undoubtedly either a fool or a knave; but those folks are too demanding.

As for our Church fathers, many in the first centuries believed that the human soul, the angels, and God were corporeal.

The world improves all the time. Saint Bernard, according to Father Mabillon's testimony,[3] taught that the soul after death did not see God in Heaven but only conversed with the humanity of Jesus Christ; his word was not enough to convince his hearers. The misadventures of the Crusades had somewhat discredited his assertions. Thousands of Scholastics succeeded him, like the Irrefutable Doctor, the Subtle Doctor, the Angelic Doctor, the Seraphic Doctor, the Cherubic Doctor,[4] all of whom were certain that they knew the soul quite clearly, but who did not hesitate to discuss it as if they hoped that no one would understand.

Our Descartes, born to uncover Antiquity's errors, if only to substitute for them his own, dragged along by that systematic spirit that blinds the greatest of men, imagined that he had demonstrated that the soul was the same thing as thought, just as matter—according to him—is the same thing as extension. He assured us that we always think, and that the soul comes to the body provided with all metaphysical ideas, knowing God, space, infinity, and having all abstract ideas—filled, in fact, with perfect knowledge, which sadly it loses as it emerges from the womb of its mother.

Mr. Malebranche, of the Oratory, in his sublime illusions, not only embraced innate ideas, but did not doubt that we see all in God, and that God, so to speak, is but our soul.

After so many thinkers had written the romance of the soul, there came a wise man who modestly described its history. Locke explained human reason to man as an excellent anatomist explains the mechanics of the human body. He used the flaming torch of physics;[5] he dared at times to speak positively, but he dared also to question; instead of instantly defining all that we do not know, he examined slowly what we wish to know. He took a child at the moment of birth; he followed step by step the progress of its understanding; he noted what it had in common with the beasts, and the ways in which it is superior to them, and above all he paid attention to his own observations, the awareness of his own ideas.

Said he, "I will leave to those who know more than I the discussion about whether the soul exists before or only after the body has been created; but I admit that the soul allotted to me is one of those coarse ones that does not always think, and I even have the misfortune to be unable to understand that it is more necessary to the soul to be thinking constantly than it is for the body to be constantly in motion."

As for me, on this matter I boast that I am as stupid as Locke. No one will ever make me believe that I am always thinking; and I am not more disposed than was he to imagine that a few weeks after my conception I had a soul full of wisdom, knowing then thousands of things that I forgot as I was being born, and that I uselessly possessed *in utero* knowledge that escaped me just when I could have used it, and that I have never been able to regain.

Having demolished innate ideas and renounced the folly of believing that we are always thinking, Locke demonstrated that all our ideas come to us through the senses, examined our simplest and most complex ideas, traced the mind of man in all its operations, and showed how imperfect are all human tongues and how we misuse terms at every turn.

He comes at last to think of the breadth, or rather the limits, of human knowledge. It is in this chapter that he dares modestly to propose: We will never, perhaps, be able to know whether a purely material being can think.

This wise remark has seemed to more than one theologian a scandalous assertion that the soul is material and mortal.

Some Englishmen, devout in their own way, sounded the alarm. Superstitious men affect society as cowards affect an army: they are filled with panic and terror and provoke it in others. Some cried that Locke wished to overturn religion, but religion did not enter into this debate; it was a purely philosophical matter, completely independent of faith and revelation; it was simply a question of examining, without bitterness, whether there is some contradiction between saying *matter can think* and *God can make matter capable of thought*.[6] But too often theologians begin by saying that God is insulted if one does not agree with them. They are too much like the bad poets who, because Despréaux was mocking them, insisted that he was insulting the king.[7]

Doctor Stillingfleet gained a reputation as a moderate theologian simply because he did not explicitly attack Locke.[8] He jousted with Locke and was defeated, for his reasoning was that of a rector and Locke argued as a philosopher, aware of the strength and weakness of human intelligence, and as one who used weapons whose temper he understood.

If I dared to speak after Mr. Locke about so difficult a subject, I would say: Men have disagreed about the nature and the immortality of the soul for a long time. It is impossible to demonstrate its immortality, since its nature is still in dispute, and one must understand a created being thoroughly before knowing whether or not it is immortal. Human reason alone is so incapable of demonstrating the immortality of the soul that religion was obliged to reveal this truth to us. Universal well-being requires that we believe the soul to be immortal; faith requires us so to believe: nothing more is needed, and the matter has been decided. The same cannot be said of the nature of the soul. Religion does not care what substance it is made of as long as it is virtuous; it is a clock given to us to regulate, but the maker did not tell us what the gears are made of.

I am a body and I think; I know no more. Shall I attribute to some unknown cause what I can so easily explain by the only secondary cause that I know? Here all the Scholastics stop me, arguing and saying: "The body consists only of extension and solidity, and it can have only movement and form. Now, movement and form, extension and solidity cannot make a thought, thus the soul cannot be material." All this fine argument, so often repeated, can be summed up thus: "I do not know what matter is; I can guess at some of its properties. Now I do not in the least know whether these properties can be joined to thought; thus, because I know nothing, I positively assert that matter cannot think." This clearly is Scholastic reasoning. Locke would modestly say to these gentlemen, "Admit at least that you are as ignorant as I, that neither your imagination nor mine can conceive how a body can have ideas; and are you then better able to understand how any substance, whatever it may be, can have ideas? You know neither matter nor spirit; how dare you to assert something?"

The superstitious come next and say that we must, for the sake of their souls, burn those who suspect that one can think with the body alone. But what would they say if it were they to be condemned for heresy? Indeed, unless he was possessed by impious folly, who would dare to assert that the Creator is incapable of giving to matter both thought and feeling? Behold, I pray you, the difficulties to which you subject yourselves, you who dare to put limits on the power of the Creator! Animals have the same organs as we, the same feelings, the same perceptions; they have memory, they can put some thoughts together. If God were not able to animate matter and give it feelings, one thing or the other must be true: either that animals are simply machines, or that they have a true soul.[9]

It seems to me almost proven that animals are not simply machines. Here is my proof: God gave them precisely the same organs of sense as ours; thus, if they feel no sensations, God has made something useless. Now God, you claim, does nothing in vain; thus He cannot have made so many organs of sense if they were not capable of sensation; therefore animals cannot be purely machines.

Animals, you say, cannot have a spiritual soul; thus, despite your claim, nothing can be said save that God gave to the organs of animals, which are simply material, the faculties of sense and perception, which in them you name "instinct."

Eh! Who can prevent God from giving our more refined organs those faculties of sensation, of perception, and of thought, which we call human reason? Whichever way you turn, you must admit your ignorance and the immense power of the Creator. Do not rebel against Locke's wise and modest philosophy. Far from attacking religion, it would serve as a support for religion, if religion needed one; for what philosophy could be more religious than one that asserts only what it clearly understands while it admits its weakness, and that tells you that we must refer to God when we examine first principles?

Moreover, one must never fear that any philosophical opinions can damage a nation's religion. Our mysteries may well contradict our proofs; they are no less revered by Christian philosophers who know that matters of reason and of faith are very different things. Philosophers will never become a religious sect. Why? Because they do not write for the masses and are dispassionate.

Divide the human race into twenty groups. Nineteen of these will be composed of those who work with their hands and will never know that there is a Locke in this world; in the twentieth group, how few there are who read! And of those readers, there are twenty who read novels for one who studies philosophy. The number of those who think is excessively small, and those who do, do not aim to disturb the world.

Montaigne, Locke, Bayle, Spinoza, Hobbes, My Lord Shaftesbury, Mr. Collins, Tolland, etc.[10]—none of these carried the torch of dissent into their lands; rather, that was done by the theologians who, beginning with the desire to be the leader of a sect, then desired to be the leaders of political parties. What am I saying! All the books of modern philosophers together will not cause as much trouble in the world as did the Franciscan monks in their disputes about the proper shapes of their sleeves and hoods.

FOURTEENTH LETTER

On Descartes and Newton

A Frenchman arriving in London finds changes in philosophy as in other matters. He left a universe that was filled; he discovers the void; in Paris, they imagine a universe composed of vortices of subtle matter; in London none of this; we think it is the pressure of the moon that causes the fluctuation of the tides; the English believe that the ocean gravitates toward the moon; so that when you think the moon should produce a high tide, these gentlemen believe you should see a low tide, which, alas, cannot be verified, because to do so one would have had to examine the moon and the tides at the moment of creation.

You will also notice that the sun, which in France has nothing to do with all this, is in London responsible for roughly a quarter of it. Your Cartesians[1] believe that everything happens by an impulse that one scarcely understands; for Mr. Newton, the cause is an attraction whose cause is no better understood. In Paris, the earth is shaped like a melon; in London, it is flattened at both ends. Light, for a Cartesian, exists in the air; for a Newtonian, it comes from the sun in six minutes and a half. Chemistry in Paris is based on acids, alkalis, and subtle matter; English chemistry is dominated by this same theory of attraction.

Even the essence of things is totally different: no one will agree either on the definition of the soul or that of matter. Descartes assures us that the soul is the same thing as thought, and Locke quite adequately proves the opposite.

Descartes insists that extension alone is the essence of matter; Newton adds solidity to this. These are dreadful contradictions.

Non nostrum inter vos tantas componere lites.[2]

This famous Newton, who destroyed the Cartesian system, died in the month of March of last year, 1727. He lived honored by his compatriots and was buried like a king who had done his subjects much good.

Here his works are read avidly, and the eulogy delivered by M. de Fontenelle[3] in the Academy of Sciences has been translated into

English. In England they expected that Mr. Fontenelle's pronouncement would provide a solemn assertion of the superiority of English philosophy, but when they saw that he compared Descartes to Newton the whole Royal Society of London rose up in arms. Far from accepting this judgment, they criticized the speech. Indeed, several members (not the most philosophical) were shocked by this comparison, simply because Descartes was French.

One must acknowledge that these two great men were very different in their conduct, their fortunes, and their philosophy.

Descartes was born with a lively and strong imagination, which made him a man as singular in his private life as he was in his manner of reasoning. This imagination could not be disguised even in his philosophical works, wherein there are ingenious and brilliant comparisons at every turn; nature had almost made him a poet, and in fact he did compose an entertainment in verse for the Queen of Sweden, which, to protect his honor, has not been printed.[4]

For a time he tried the military profession,[5] and after that, having entirely become a philosopher, he thought it not unworthy of him to be a lover. He had by his mistress a daughter named Francine who died young and whose loss he felt deeply; and thus he experienced all of human life.

He thought for a long while that, to philosophize freely, he had to fly from mankind and especially from his country. He was right; the men of his time knew too little to enlighten him and were at best able only to harm him.

He left France because he sought truth, which was persecuted there by the miserable philosophy of the Scholastics; but he found little better in the universities of Holland to which he withdrew. For at the time when the French condemned in his philosophy the only propositions that were true, he was also persecuted by the so-called philosophers of Holland who understood him no better and who, more closely acquainted with his reputation, hated his person still more. He was obliged to leave Utrecht; he was subjected to the accusation of atheism, that last resort of calumny; and he, who had used all the wisdom of his mind to find new proofs of the existence of a God, was suspected of refusing to recognize His existence.

So many persecutions presuppose great merit and a dazzling reputation; indeed, he had both. Reason was to some extent able to break through the fog of Scholasticism and the prejudices of popular opinion and enter the world. Descartes' name made such a stir that the French wanted to entice him back with rewards. They promised a pension of a thousand crowns; he came with this expectation; he himself paid for his commission, which in those days was for sale, but did not receive the pension and returned to Northern Holland to philosophize in solitude at the same time that the great Galileo, at the age of eighty, languished in the prison of the Inquisition for having demonstrated the earth's movement.[6] Surrounded by scholars who were his enemies, in the hands of a physician who hated him, he died a premature death caused by an unhealthy life.

The life of Milord Newton was completely different. He lived for eighty-five years, tranquil, happy, and honored by his country.

His great good fortune was to have been born in a free country, in a time when Scholastic foolishness had been banished and reason alone was cultivated, so that the world could not but be his student rather than his enemy.

One extraordinary contrast between himself and Descartes is that in the course of so long a life he felt neither passion nor weakness; he had never been intimate with a woman: this was confirmed by the doctor and the surgeon in whose arms he died. One might admire Newton for this, but one ought not to reproach Descartes.

Public opinion in England about these two philosophers asserts that the former was a dreamer and the other a sage.

Very few in London read Descartes, whose works have in effect become useless; very few read Newton because one must be very learned to understand him. Yet everyone talks of them; no credit is given to the Frenchman and all to the Englishman. Some believe that if one no longer fears the void, if one knows that air has weight, if one uses a telescope, one does so thanks to Newton. He plays the role of Hercules in the fable, to whom the ignorant attribute all the deeds of other heroes.

A British critique of M. de Fontenelle's discourse dared to suggest that Descartes was not a great geometer. Those who speak this way might be accused of attacking their nurses. From the point at which he found geometry to the point at which he left it, Descartes traveled as far as did Newton after him; he is the first who found a way to formulate algebraic equations to describe curves. His geometry, which today is universally known, was in his time so profound that no professor dared to explicate it, and only Schooten in Holland and Fermat in France understood it.[7]

He applied this geometric and inventive ability to the field of optics and lens making, which became in his hands an entirely new art, and if he did err in some respects, it is because someone who discovers a new world cannot in one glance know all its properties; those who come after him and who render these lands fertile owe to him at least the thanks for discovering it. I will not deny, however, that other works by M. Descartes swarm with errors.

Geometry is a guide that he to some extent created, and which would have guided him faithfully in his study of physics; yet finally he abandoned this guide and surrendered to the desire for system. At this point his philosophy became no more than an ingenious tale, at most merely plausible for ignorant people. He mistook the nature of the soul, the proofs of the existence of God, the nature of matter, the laws of movement, and the nature of light; he believed in innate ideas, he invented new elements, he created a world, he made man in his image, and with good reason is it said that man according to Descartes is simply Descartes' man, very far from man as he really is.

He pushed his metaphysical mistakes so far as to insist that two and two make four only because God wished it thus. Yet it is not too much to say that even in his mistakes he is admirable; he erred, but it was at least systematically and with consistency. He demolished the absurd fantasies with which children have been entertained these past two thousand years; he taught the men of his time to reason, and even to use his own weapons against him. If he did not use true coinage, he at least denounced the counterfeit.

I do not think one could properly compare his philosophy with that of Newton; the first is a rough sketch, the second is a masterpiece. But he who put us on the path to truth is perhaps worth as much as is he who later traveled to the end.

Descartes gave sight to the blind, and they saw the mistakes of Antiquity as well as his own. The path he opened up has since become immense. For a while the little book by Rohault[8] presented a complete account of physics; today, all the collected works of the European academies are not even the beginning of systematic thinking: efforts to fathom the abyss revealed that it is infinitely deep. Now we must see what M. Newton has found in its depths.

FIFTEENTH LETTER

On the System of Attraction

The discoveries of Lord Newton, which gave him universal fame, concern the system of the world, light, the infinite in geometry, and, finally, the chronology of the world, with which he entertained himself as a relaxation.

I will tell you (if I can do so, concisely) the little I have been able to understand of these sublime ideas.

With regard to the system of our world, for a long time there was much dispute about the force that turns the planets and keeps them in their orbits, and about what causes all things here below to fall to the surface of the earth.

Descartes' system, explained and much changed since his day, seemed to present a plausible explanation for these phenomena, and the simplicity and intelligibility of this explanation made it appear all the more valid. But in philosophical matters one must be wary both of what one understands too easily and of what one does not understand at all.

Weight, the acceleration of bodies falling to the earth, the revolution of planets in their orbits, their rotation on their axes, all that is simply movement; now, movement can only be understood by propulsion, thus, all bodies are propelled. But what propels them? All space is full; thus it is filled with matter that must be very rarified since we cannot perceive it; this matter must move from Occident to Orient, since all the planets are pulled from Occident to Orient. Thus, from hypothesis to hypothesis and from appearance to appearance, a great vortex of subtle matter is proposed, by which the planets are dragged around the sun; and another vortex that turns inside the larger one and that turns each day about the planet. Once all this is imagined, it is assumed that weight depends on this daily movement, for, it is said, the subtle matter that turns around our little vortex must go seventeen times faster than the earth. Now, if it goes seventeen times faster than the earth, it must have incomparably greater centrifugal force and must therefore push all bodies toward the earth. This is the explanation of weight in the Cartesian system.

But before calculating this centrifugal force and the speed of this subtle matter, it was necessary to be sure that it exists; and even were it to exist, it has nonetheless been proven that this could not be the cause of weight.

Mr. Newton seems to have completely destroyed all these large and small vortices, both the one that carries the planets around the sun and that which makes each planet revolve on its axis.

First, with respect to the earth and its supposed smaller vortex, it has been demonstrated that it must lose its movement little by little. It has been demonstrated that if the earth swims in some fluid, this fluid must have the same density as the earth; and that if this fluid is of the same density, all the things that we move must suffer enormous resistance—that is, one would need a lever as large as the earth to lift a single pound.

Second, the greater vortices are even more illusory. It is impossible to make them consistent with Kepler's laws, whose validity has been demonstrated. Mr. Newton has shown that the revolution of the fluid by which Jupiter is assumed to be dragged does not coincide with the movement of the earth's fluid, as Jupiter's revolution coincides with that of the earth.[1]

He proves that, since all planets make their revolutions in ellipses and thus are much farther from each other in their aphelia than in their perihelia, the earth, for example, should go more quickly when it is near Venus and Mars, since the fluid that drags it, being more compressed, should have more motion; yet it is just at this time that the earth moves the slowest.

He proves that there is no celestial matter that moves from Occident to Orient, since at times comets cross these spaces from Orient to Occident, and sometimes from North to South.

And to cut through all difficulties still further, if that were possible, he proves or at least argues strongly on the basis of experiments that the *plenum* [in the universe] is impossible, and returns to us the void that Aristotle and Descartes had banished.

Having by these arguments and many more demolished the Cartesian vortices, he despaired of ever knowing whether there was a hidden force in nature that could cause both the movements of the heavenly bodies and the weight of things on earth. In 1666 he withdrew to the countryside near Cambridge; walking one day in his garden and seeing fruit falling from a tree, he fell into a profound meditation on this question of weight, the cause of which philosophers had so long sought in vain and whose mysterious nature ordinary men never suspected.[2] He said to himself, "From whatever height in our hemisphere these bodies might fall, their rate of fall will certainly be that discovered by Galileo; and the space through which they fall will be proportionate to the square of the time in which they fall. This power that makes objects fall remains the same without any perceptible diminution, whether one is in the lowlands or high upon a mountain. Why would not this power extend up to the moon? And if it is true that it extends to the moon, does it not seem that this power keeps the moon in its orbit and determines its movement? But if the moon obeys this principle, whatever it may be, is it not reasonable to believe that the other planets are equally subject to it?

"If this force exists, it must (and this also has been proven) grow in inverse proportion to the square of the distances. Thus we need only examine the trajectory of a heavy body falling to earth from a modest height, and the trajectory traced by a body falling from the orbit of the moon in the same amount of time. And to learn this we need only to know the size of the earth and the distance from the moon to the earth."

Thus reasoned Mr. Newton. But in England at that time there were only very inaccurate measurements of the globe; these were based on uncertain estimates of mariners who counted sixty English miles to one degree of latitude, whereas the distance was in fact close to seventy miles. Since this mistaken calculation did not fit Mr. Newton's conclusions, he abandoned them. A mediocre and arrogant philosopher would have accommodated the measurements to his system as best as he could. Mr. Newton preferred to abandon his project. But from the moment that M. Picard[3] had, to the glory of France, measured the earth exactly by establishing the meridian, Mr. Newton again took up his first hypothesis and found he was justified by the calculations of M. Picard. It has always seemed admirable to me that such sublime truths have been discovered with the help of a quadrant and a bit of arithmetic.

The circumference of the earth is one hundred and twenty-three million, two hundred forty-nine thousand, and six hundred Parisian feet.[4] This fact alone is the basis for the whole system of Attraction.[5]

We know the circumference of the earth; we know the circumference of the orbit of the moon and the diameter of this orbit. The moon revolves in this orbit in twenty-seven days, seven hours, forty-three minutes; thus it is demonstrated that the moon, in its mean motion, traverses one hundred eighty-seven thousand, nine hundred and sixty Parisian feet per minute; and a well-known theorem has demonstrated that the fundamental force that would make an object fall from the height of the moon would make it fall only fifteen Parisian feet in the first minute.

Now, if it is true that bodies have weight, fall, and attract each other in inverse proportion to the squares of the distances, and if the same force operates the same way throughout all nature, it is clear that since the earth is sixty half-diameters from the moon, a heavy body must fall to earth fifteen feet in the first second and fifty-four thousand feet in the first minute.

Now, it is true that a heavy body in fact falls fifteen feet in the first second and covers in the first minute fifty-four thousand feet, which number is the square of sixty multiplied by fifteen; thus the weight of the bodies is in inverse proportion to the squares of the distance, and thus the same force accounts for weight on earth and the stability of the moon in its orbit.

Since it has been demonstrated that the moon weighs on the earth, which is the center of its own movement, it has been demonstrated that the earth and the moon weigh on the sun, which is the center of their annual movement.

The other planets must be subject to this general law, and, if this law exists, these planets must follow the laws discovered by Kepler. All these laws, all these relations, are in fact maintained by the planets with the greatest precision; thus the force of gravity attracts all the planets toward the sun, as it does for our own globe. Finally, the reaction of each body being proportionate to its action, it is then certain that the earth attracts and is attracted by the moon, and that the sun attracts and is attracted by both, that each satellite of Saturn attracts and is attracted by the other four, and that all five attract and are attracted by Saturn; that the same is true for Jupiter, and that all these globes are drawn to and draw upon the sun.

This power of gravity operates in proportion to the matter that each body contains; this is a truth that M. Newton has demonstrated by experiments. The new discovery has shown that the sun, at the center of all the planets, attracts them all in direct relation to their mass and their distance. Thus, mounting by degrees to insights that seemed unattainable to human intelligence, he dares to calculate how much matter the sun contains and how much makes up each planet; and thus he shows, by simple rules of mechanics, that each celestial orb must necessarily be in the place where it is. The laws of gravitation alone explain all the apparent irregularities that appear in the paths of the celestial orbs. The phases of the moon are the necessary consequences of these laws. Moreover, we see plainly why the nodes of the moon revolve in nineteen years and those of the earth require about twenty-six thousand years. The flux and reflux of the sea are simply the results of this Attraction. The closeness of the moon when it is full and when it is new, and its greater distance from the earth in the first and third quarters, combined with the action of the sun, give a clear explanation of the rise and fall of the sea.

Having explained by his sublime theory the orbits and variations of the planets' motion, he harnessed the comets by the same law. These fires, so long incomprehensible, the terror of the world and the stumbling block of philosophers, placed by Aristotle below the moon and relegated by Descartes beyond Saturn, are now put in their true place by Newton.

He proves that they are solid bodies, that they move within the sphere of the sun, and describe an ellipse so eccentric and so close to a parabola that some comets require more than five hundred years to complete their revolution.

M. Halley[6] believes that the comet of 1680 is the same one that appeared in the time of Julius Caesar. This one in particular serves to show that comets are solid and opaque, for it came so close to the sun that it was only a sixth part of its disk in its distance from the sun; it must, therefore, have been heated to a temperature two thousand times greater than that of the hottest iron. It would have been dissolved and burned up in very little time if it had not been a solid body. It was then becoming fashionable to determine the trajectory of comets. The celebrated mathematician Jacques Bernoulli concluded by his theory that the famous comet of 1680 would appear on the 17th of May 1719. Not one European astronomer went to bed on the night of the 17th of May, but the famous comet did not appear. It would have been more apt, if not indeed more accurate, to allow it five hundred and seventy-five years in which to return. An English geometer named Whiston,[7] a crackbrain as well as a geometer, seriously affirmed that at the moment of the Flood there had been a comet that had inundated our globe, and he was unjustly astonished when people mocked him. The ancient world thought more or less as Whiston did; it believed that comets were always the heralds of some great misfortune to befall the earth. Newton, on the other hand, suspected that comets were benign, and that the fumes that came from them helped and revived those planets that, in their orbits, soaked up all those particles that the sun detached from the comets. This notion is at the least more probable than the other.

Nor is this all. If this gravitational force, this Attraction, operates on all the celestial bodies, it doubtless works on all the parts of these bodies; for if bodies attract one another in proportion to their masses, it can only be because of the total of their individual parts; and if this power is lodged within the whole, it is doubtless in the half, in the quarter, in the eighth part, and so to infinity. Moreover, if this force were not equally distributed throughout, there would always be some parts of the world that exert greater gravitational force than others, which does not occur. Thus the force really exists in all matter and in the smallest particle of matter.

Thus, Attraction is the great source of movement in all of nature.

Having demonstrated the existence of this force, Newton indeed anticipated that there would be objections to the word itself. In more than one passage of his book he warned his reader about the idea of Attraction, urging him not to confuse this idea with the occult forces described in Antiquity, and to be willing simply to recognize that there is in each body a central force that, from one end of the universe to the other, influences, by the immutable laws of mechanics, the closest as well as the most remote bodies.

It is astonishing that, after the solemn warnings of this great philosopher, M. Saurin and M. de Fontenelle, who also deserve to be called philosophers, should have accused him point-blank of supporting the delusions of the Aristotelians—M. Saurin in the *Mémoires de l'Académie* of 1709, and M. de Fontenelle in his own *Eloge* of Mr. Newton.[8]

Almost all the French, scholars and others, have repeated this rebuke. One hears everywhere, "Why did not Newton make use of the word 'impulse,' which we understand so clearly, rather than using the word 'Attraction,' which we do not understand?"

Newton could have answered his critics thus: "First, you understand the word 'impulse' no better than you understand the word 'Attraction,' and if you cannot imagine why a body moves toward the center of another body, neither can you understand by what means one body pushes another.

"Secondly, I could not accept 'impulse,' for, to do this, I would have had to know for certain that some celestial matter in fact pushes the planets; now, not only do I not recognize such matter, but I have proven that it does not exist.

"Third, I only use the word 'Attraction' to express an effect that I have observed in nature, a certain and indisputable effect of an unknown principle, a quality inherent in matter the cause of which others more adept than I may perhaps discover."

"What then have you taught us?" they insist once again, "and why so many calculations to tell us about something that you yourself do not understand?"

"I have taught you," Newton might continue, "that the mechanics of this central force gives weight to objects in proportion to their mass, that this central force alone moves the planets and the comets in their evident relations. I have demonstrated that there cannot be any other cause of weight and movement in celestial bodies; for, since heavy bodies fall to earth according to the obvious effects of the central force and the planets continue in their orbits according to the same effects, if there were yet another force that works on all these bodies, it would increase their speed or change their direction. Now, not one of these bodies has a single degree of movement, of speed, of direction that cannot be proved to be the effect of this central force; thus it is impossible that there be any other."

Let me allow Newton to speak for another moment. Would it not be proper for him to say, "I am in a different position from the Ancients. They saw, let us say, water raised by pumps and said, 'Water rises because it has a horror of the void.' But I am in the situation of one who was the first to notice that water is raised by pumps, and who leaves it to others to explain the cause of this effect. The anatomist who first said that the arm moves because muscles contract taught men an incontestable truth; would one be less obliged to him because he did not know why the muscles contract? The cause of air pressure is unknown, but the one who discovered this pressure did a great service to physics. The force that I discovered is more hidden and more universal; thus I should the more be thanked. I have discovered a new property of matter, one of the Creator's secrets; I have calculated it and demonstrated its effects; should I be tormented because of the name I gave it?

"One might accuse the vortices of being occult, since no one has proven their existence. Attraction, on the other hand, is something real, since we have demonstrated its effects and calculated its proportions. The cause of this cause lies hidden in God's bosom." *Procedes huc, et non ibis amplius.*[9]

SIXTEENTH LETTER

On Mr. Newton's Optics

A new universe was discovered by the philosophers [scientists] of the last century, and this new world was all the more difficult to understand because no one had suspected that it existed. To the wisest, it seemed like arrogance even to dare to think that one could learn the laws by which the celestial bodies move and how light behaves.

Galileo by his astronomical discoveries, Kepler by his calculations, Descartes at least in his *Dioptrique*,[1] and Newton in all his works, saw the mechanics of the springs that move the world. Geometry reduced the infinite to the calculable. Understanding the circulation of blood in animals and sap in plants changed nature for us. A new way of existing was imposed on bodies in pneumatic machines; objects were brought closer to our eyes by means of telescopes; finally, after such new discoveries, what Newton learned about light rivals anything attained by the most audacious human curiosity.

Until Antonio de Dominis,[2] the rainbow seemed an inexplicable miracle; this philosopher understood that it was a necessary effect of rain and sun. Descartes made his name immortal by the mathematical explications of this natural phenomenon; he calculated the angles of reflection of light in drops of rain, and his intelligence seemed to partake of the divine.

But what would he have said if he had learned that he was wrong about the nature of light? That there was no reason to insist that it has the nature of a particle? That it is false to assume that this matter, which exists throughout the universe, only requires for its action that it be pushed by the sun, as one end of a long stick wavers when the other is pushed? That it is very true that it is darted out of the sun? And finally, that light is transmitted from the sun to the earth in about seven minutes, although a cannon ball, even if it maintained its speed, could only accomplish this in twenty-five years? What would his astonishment have been if someone had told him: "It is not true the light reflects directly when it bounces off the solid parts of bodies; it is not true that bodies are transparent when they have large pores; and a man will appear who will demonstrate [the truth behind] these paradoxes and who will dissect a single ray of light with more dexterity than the most skillful anatomist can dissect a human body."

This man has come. Newton, using only a prism, demonstrated to the eye that light is a combination of colored rays that, combined, produce white light. He divided one single ray into seven bands, which appeared in order on a white cloth or paper, one above the other, and at unequal distances. The first is the color of fire; the second, orange; the third yellow; the fourth, green; the fifth, blue; the sixth, indigo; the seventh, violet. Each of these bands, even if spread out by a hundred other prisms, will never change its color, any more than pure gold will change in a crucible; and to give added proof that each of these bands of color carries in itself the quality that makes its color, take a little bit of yellow wood and shine the red band upon it and the wood will take on the red color; shine on it the green band and the wood will take on that color, and so on.

What then is the cause of color in nature? Simply the nature of the body that disposes it to reflect some bands of light and absorb others. What is this secret quality? Newton showed that it is simply the thickness of the little particles that make up a body. And how is this reflection produced? Hitherto people thought it was because the rays of light rebounded the way a ball rebounds from a solid surface. Not at all: Newton taught the astonished philosophers that bodies are opaque only because their pores are large, that light is reflected to our eyes from the interior of these pores, that the smaller the pores, the more transparent the body; thus paper that reflects light when it is dry, transmits it when it is soaked in oil because the oil, filling the pores, makes them smaller.

Thus, examining the great porosity of bodies, each part having pores, and each part of its part having its own pores, Newton showed that it is not certain that there is a cubic inch of solid matter in the universe; how far then is our mind from understanding what matter truly is!

Having thus dissected light, and having carried the wisdom of his discoveries so far as to demonstrate how we know the color that is formed by all the primitive colors, he showed that these elementary bands of color separated by the prism are arranged in their order because they are refracted in this order; and this hitherto unknown property of light to break up into these unequal bands of color, this power of refracting red less than orange, etc., this is what he calls refrangibility.

The bands of color that are most reflective are those that are the most refrangible; and thus he demonstrated that the same power causes both reflection and refraction of light.

All these wonders are but the beginning of his discoveries; he discovered the secret of seeing the vibrations and shocks of light that come and go endlessly and that transmit or reflect light depending on the density of the bodies that it hits; he dared to calculate the density of air particles between two lenses, one flat, one convex on one side, and placed upon one another, that is needed to cause transmission or reflection of light, and to make visible different colors.

From all these combinations he discovered the extent to which light acts on solid bodies and the way the bodies affect it.

He understood light so well that he was able to determine the limits on the effectiveness of telescopes.

Descartes, inspired by an understandable and noble self-confidence engendered by the beginnings of knowledge for which he was responsible, hoped that, using a telescope, one could see in the stars objects as small as those that we can discern on earth.

Newton showed that telescopes cannot be made perfect because of this refraction and refrangibility that, while they make objects appear closer, spread out the individual bands of light; he calculated in these lenses the proportion of separation between the red and blue bands; and, pursuing the examination of matters whose very existence no one suspected, he examined the inequalities that the shape of the lens produces, and the one that produces refrangibility. He found that when the objective lens of the telescope is convex on one side and flat on the other, if the flat side is turned toward the object, the distortion that comes from the construction and position of the lens is five thousand times less than the distortion produced by the refractivity; and that therefore it is not because of the shape of the lenses that one cannot perfect a telescope, but because of the nature of light itself.

This is why he invented a telescope that works by reflection rather than by refraction. This new kind of glass is very hard to make and not easy to use; but in England it is said that a reflective telescope that is five feet long is as powerful as [a refractive] one a hundred feet in length.

Seventeenth Letter

On Infinity and on Chronology

The labyrinth and abyss of the infinite is another territory explored by Newton, and he gave us the thread by which we can find our way through it.

Descartes once again is his precursor in this astonishing new world; his geometry allowed him to take long strides towards the infinite, but he stopped at its edge. Mr. Wallis, in the middle of the last century, was the first to reduce a fraction, by perpetual division, to an infinite series.[1]

Lord Brouncker used this series to calculate the area of the hyperbola.[2]

Mercator published a demonstration of this calculation.[3] It was at about this time that Newton, at the age of twenty-three, invented a general method to apply the calculations for the hyperbola to all curves.

This method of submitting the infinite to algebraic calculation is called differential calculus, or the calculus of fluxions, and also integral calculus.[4] It is the art of numbering and measuring exactly things whose existence one cannot even imagine.

Indeed, would you not think that someone was mocking you if he said that there are lines of infinite length that form an infinitely small angle?

That a straight line is straight as long as it is finite, and that, changing its direction an infinitely small amount, it becomes an infinite curve, and that a curve can become infinitely less curved?

That there are squares of infinity, cubes of infinity, infinities of infinity, [in a series of which] the penultimate one is as nothing compared to the last one?

All of this, which at first seems the height of unreason, is the finest and most extensive use of human intelligence, and a method of finding truths that were hitherto unknown.

This daring construction is even based on simple ideas. It is simply a question of measuring the diagonal of a square, of knowing the area of a curve, of finding for some number a square root that cannot be determined by ordinary arithmetic.

And after all, so many orders of infinity should not be more distressing to the imagination than this well-known proposition, that between a circle and a tangent one can always insert curved lines; or this other, that matter is always divisible. These two truths have long since been demonstrated and are no more comprehensible than the others.

Many have challenged whether Newton did invent this famous calculus. In Germany Mr. Leibniz is said to be the inventor of the differentials, which Newton calls fluxions, and Bernoulli claims the integral calculus; but the honor of the first discovery remains with Newton, and to the others is left only the glory of being considered together with him.[5]

In the same way Harvey's discovery of the circulation of the blood[6] was challenged, and M. Perrault's discovery of the circulation of sap in plants.[7] Hartsoeker and Leeuwenhoek both claimed to have been the first to see the little worms of which we are made. This same Hartsoeker[8] challenged M. Huygens' claim of inventing a new way of calculating the distance to a fixed star. We do not yet know which philosopher solved the problem of the cycloid.[9]

However it may be, Newton came to the most sublime knowledge by means of his geometry of the infinite.

Yet to be described is another accomplishment more accessible to the human mind, but which also reflects the creative spirit that Newton brought to all his research: it is an entirely new chronology, for, in all that he undertook, he had always to change the received opinions of other men.[10]

Accustomed to disentangling chaos, he wanted to shed a little light on those ancient fables that are interwoven with history and to establish a clear chronology. It is true that there is no family, city, or nation that does not wish to establish its antiquity. Moreover, the first historians are the most careless about dates; books were a thousand times less common than they are today. Consequently, there being less opportunity for criticism, it was easier to deceive others with impunity; and since the events were obviously invented, it is probable that the dates were as well.

In general, it seemed to Newton that the world was five hundred years younger than the chronologists asserted; he based his ideas on the ordinary course of nature and on astronomical observation.

By the ordinary course of nature we mean the span of each human generation. The Egyptians were the first to use this uncertain method of counting. When they wanted to write of the beginnings of their history, they counted three hundred and forty-one generations from Menes to Sethon;[11] and having no fixed dates, they calculated that there were three generations in a century; thus they assumed that between the reign of Menes and the reign of Sethon there were eleven thousand three hundred and forty years.

The Greeks, before they counted time by Olympiads,[12] used the same method as the Egyptians and slightly extended the length of a generation, stretching each one to forty years.

Now in this respect the Egyptians and the Greeks were mistaken in their calculations. It is true that in nature three generations ordinarily account for about one hundred to one hundred and twenty years, but only rarely do three reigns account for the same number of years. It is very evident that in general men live longer than kings reign. Thus, a man who would write history without having precise dates, and who knows there were nine kings in a nation, would be very wrong to assume that these nine kings reigned for three hundred years. Each generation is about thirty-six years long; each reign is about twenty, if their reigns succeed one another directly. Take the thirty kings of England, from William the Conqueror to George I: they reigned six hundred forty-eight years, which, divided among the thirty kings, gives each a reign of twenty-one and a half years. Sixty-three kings reigned in France, one after the other, each reigning about twenty years. This is the ordinary course of nature. Thus the Ancients were mistaken when they assumed that a reign was the equal of a generation; thus they counted too many years; thus it is proper to subtract something from their calculations.

Astronomical observations seem to have been of greater help to our philosopher; he seems more sure of himself fighting on his own field.

You know, Sir, that the earth, in addition to its annual motion, which carries it around the sun from west to east in the course of a year, has also another curious revolution, altogether unknown until recently. The poles have a very slow retrograde motion from east to west, which means that on each day their position does not correspond precisely to the same part of the sky. This difference, undetectable in a year, becomes quite pronounced with time, and at the end of seventy-two years we find that the difference amounts to one degree, that is to say, to the three hundred and sixtieth part of all the sky. Thus, after seventy-two years, the colure[13] of the spring equinox, which formerly intersected a fixed [star], now intersects a different one. Thus the sun, rather than being in the part of the zodiac called Aries, the Ram, in the time of Hipparchos, now finds itself in the region of Taurus, the Bull; and Gemini, the Twins are where

Taurus once was. All the astronomical constellations have changed their place, yet we retain the old vocabulary; we say that the sun is in Aries in the spring, just as we continue to say that the sun rises and sets.

Hipparchus was the first of the Greeks who noticed some changes in the relationship between the constellations and the equinoxes, or rather he learned this from the Egyptians. The philosophers attributed this movement to the stars, for in those days they were far from imagining such a revolution in the earth, which they thought was motionless in all respects. Thus they invented a heaven to which they attached all the stars, and gave this heaven a special movement that made it move eastward, while the daily movement of all the stars seemed to be from east to west. To this error they added another more important one: they thought that the heaven of the fixed stars moved eastward by one degree every hundred years, thus they were as mistaken in their astronomical calculations as they were in their observations of the natural world. For example, an astronomer would have said, "The spring equinox was, in the time of such an observer, in such a sign of the zodiac, at such a star; the distance from that observer to us is two degrees; two degrees equal two hundred years; thus this observer lived two hundred years before me." It is certain that an astronomer who reasoned thus would have miscalculated by fifty-four years. This is why the Ancients, doubly mistaken, calculated the Great Year, that is, one revolution of the whole sky, to be about thirty-six thousand years. But the Moderns know that this imagined revolution of the heaven of fixed stars is simply the revolution of the earth's poles, which happens in the course of twenty-five thousand, nine hundred years. We should note in passing that Newton, in determining the figure[14] of the earth, has neatly explained the reasons for this revolution.

All this having been stated, to establish a chronology it was necessary to identify the fixed star that today marks the place where the colure of the spring equinox intersects the ecliptic, and to know whether some Ancient stated at what point, in relation to a star, the ecliptic was intersected by the same colure of the equinoxes.

Clement of Alexandria reports that Chiron, one of the Argonauts, observed the constellations in the course of that famous expedition, and set the spring equinox in the middle of the sign of Aries; the autumn equinox in the middle of the sign of Libra, the Scales; the summer solstice in the middle of Cancer, the Crab; and the winter solstice in the middle of Capricorn, the Goat.

Long after the voyage of the Argo, one year before the Peloponnesian War,[15] Meton observed that the summer solstice passed through the eighth degree of Cancer.

Now, each sign of the zodiac occupies thirty degrees. In the time of Chiron, the solstice was half-way through the sign, at fifteen degrees; one year before the Peloponnesian War it was at the eighth degree; thus it had regressed seven degrees. One degree is equivalent to seventy-two years: thus, from the beginning of the Peloponnesian War to the voyage of the Argonauts, there were seven times seventy-two years, or five hundred and four years, and not the seven hundred that the Greeks claimed. Thus, comparing the sky of today with the sky as it was then, we see that the voyage of the Argonauts must have taken place about nine hundred, rather than fourteen hundred, years before Jesus Christ; and therefore, the world is about five hundred years less old than previously believed. Thus all the epochs are closer to one another, and everything happened later than was supposed. I do not know whether this ingenious explanation will be widely accepted, and whether, on the basis of these ideas, one would wish to recalculate the chronology of the world. Perhaps the savants will find it too much honor for one man to have perfected physics, geometry, and history; it would be a kind of absolute monarchy that their pride would ill accept. Thus, in the days when great philosophers attacked Newton for his theory of Attraction, others disputed his chronological system. Time, which should reveal whose is the victory, may perhaps only leave the issue more undecided.

EIGHTEENTH LETTER

On Tragedy

The English already had theater, as did the Spanish, when the French only had traveling players.[1] Shakespeare, who was, so to speak, the English Corneille, flowered in the days of Lope de Vega; he created the true theater.[2] His genius was strong and fertile, full of nature and the sublime, without the slightest spark of good taste, and without the least understanding of the rules. I will tell you something daring but true: The great accomplishments of this author doomed English theater; he gave us such beautiful scenes, such great and terrible moments sprinkled through his monstrous farces, which some call tragedies, that these plays have always been performed to great applause. Time, which alone can establish a man's reputation, has at last made those defects respectable. Most of the bizarre and monstrous inventions of this author have, after two hundred years, gained the right to be considered sublime. Most modern authors have copied them; but what worked well for Shakespeare is hissed at when they try it, and you can imagine that the homage paid to this older writer grows in proportion to the disrespect given to the modern playwrights. No one understands that one ought not to imitate him, and the failures of these imitators simply makes others believe he is inimitable.

You know that in *The Moor of Venice*, a very touching play, a husband strangles his wife on the stage, and when the poor woman is strangled she cries that she has been unjustly killed. You are aware that in *Hamlet* the gravediggers are drunk, sing tavern songs, and make jokes proper to their profession as they play with the skulls they unearth. But what will surprise you is that these follies were imitated during the reign of Charles II, an era of elegance and the golden age of the fine arts.[3]

Otway, in his *Venice Preserv'd*, inserts the courtier Antonio and the courtesan Naki in the midst of the horrors of Marquis Bedmar's conspiracy.[4] The old senator Antonio offers his courtesan all the ridiculous compliments made by all impotent foolish old men: he pretends to be a bull and a hound; he bites his mistress's legs, who kicks and whips him. These buffooneries, addressed to the vulgar mob, have been edited out of Otway, but in Shakespeare's *Julius Caesar* the jokes of the Roman shoemakers and cobblers, who are brought onto the same stage as Brutus and Cassius, have been kept. It is because Otway's foolishness is modern while Shakespeare's is ancient.

You will no doubt complain that those who have told you about English theater, and especially about this famous Shakespeare, have until now shown you only his errors, and that no one has translated those wonderful moments that excuse all his faults. I will reply that it is easy to reproduce in prose the defects of a poet, but very difficult to translate his beautiful verse. All those scribblers who set themselves up as critics of celebrated writers have filled volumes; I would prefer two pages that acquaint us with some excellence. I will always maintain, as do people who have good taste, that more is to be gained from twelve lines of Homer and Virgil than from all the critical commentaries on these two great men.

I have dared to translate a few fragments of the best English poets. Here is one by Shakespeare; be generous to the copy for the sake of the original, and remember always, when you see a translation, that you see only a poorly engraved print of a beautiful painting.

I have chosen the monologue from the tragedy of *Hamlet*, which is known by all, and which begins with this line: To be, or not to be? That is the question!

[The following is the original Shakespeare:]

To be, or not to be? that is the question:
Whether 't is nobler in the mind to suffer

[Voltaire's French, pp. 71–72, does not include the following lines of the original Shakespeare:

The slings and arrows of outrageous fortune,
Or to take arms against a sea of troubles,
And by opposing, end them? To die, to sleep—
No more, and by a sleep to say we end
The heart-ache, and the thousand natural shocks
That flesh is heir to. 'T is a consummation
Devoutly to be wished. To die, to sleep—
To sleep; perchance to dream—Ay, there's the rub;

For in that sleep of death, what dreams may come
When we have shuffled off this mortal coil,
Must give us pause. There 's the respect
That makes a calamity of so long life:
For who would bear the whips and scorns of time,
The oppressor's wrong, the proud man's contumely,
The pangs of despised love, the law's delay,
The insolence of office, and the spurns
That patient merit of the unworthy takes,
When he himself might his quietus make
With a bare bodkin. Who would fardels bear
To grunt and sweat under a weary life,
But that the dread of something after death,
The undiscovered country, from whose bourn
No traveller returns, puzzles the will, ·
And makes us rather bear those ills we have,
Than fly to others that we know not of?
Thus conscience does make cowards of us all;
And thus the native hue of resolution
Is sicklied o'er with the pale cast of thought:
And enterprises of great weight and moment
With this regard their currents turn awry,
And lose the name of action—]

[Voltaire's original French translation of Shakespeare:5]

Demeure, il faut choisir et passer à l'instant
De la vie à la mort, ou de l'être au néant.
Dieux cruels, s'il en est, éclairez mon courage.
Faut-il vieillir courbé sous la main qui m'outrage,
Supporter ou finir mon malheur et mon sort?
Qui suis je? Qui m'arrête! et qu'est-ce que la mort?
C'est la fin de nos maux, c'est mon unique asile
Après de longs transports, c'est un sommeil tranquile.
On s'endort, et tout meurt. Mais un affreux réveil
Doit succéder peut-être aux douceurs du sommeil.
On nous menace, on dit que cette courte vie,
De tourments éternels est aussi-tôt suivie.
O mort! moment fatal! affreuse éternité!
Tout cœur à ton seul nom se glace épouvanté.
Eh! qui pourroit sans toi supporter cette vie,

De nos prêtres menteurs benir l'hypocrisie;
D'une indigne maîtresse encenser les erreurs,
Ramper sous un ministre, adorer ses hauteurs;
Et montrer les langueurs de son âme abattüe,
A des amis ingrats qui detournent la vue?
La mort seroit trop douce en ces extrémitez,
Mais le scrupule parle, et nous crie, arrêtez;
Il defend à nos mains cet heureux homicide
Et d'un heros guerrier, fait un Chrétien timide &c.

Do not think I have given you the English word for word; a curse on those who concoct literal translations, and who, translating each word, destroy the meaning! Here indeed one can say that the letter killeth, and the spirit giveth life.

Here is another passage from a famous English tragedian, Dryden, a poet[6] in the time of Charles II, an author, more prolific than judicious, who would have a better reputation had he written but a tenth of his works, and whose great defect was to wish to be the universal poet.

This fragment begins thus:

[Dryden's text follows:]

When I consider life, 'tis all a cheat.
Yet fool'd by hope men favor the deceit.[7]

[Voltaire's translation of Dryden's text:]

De desseins en regrets et d'erreurs en désirs
Les mortels insensés promènent leur folie.
Dans des malheurs présents, dans l'espoir des plaisirs,
Nous ne vivons jamais, nous attendons la vie.
Demain, demain, dit-on, va combìer tous nos voeux;
Demain vient, et nous laisse encore plus malheureux.
Quelle est l'erreur, hélas! du soin qui nous dévore?
Nul de nous ne voudrait recommencer son cours:
De nos premiers moments nous maudissons l'aurore,
Et de la nuit qui vient nous attendons encore
Ce qu'ont en vain promis les plus beaux de noss jours, etc.

[English translation of Voltaire's French translation of Dryden:

From plans to regrets, from errors to desires,
Insane mortals parade their folly.
In present misery, in the hope of pleasure
We never live, we wait for life.
Tomorrow, tomorrow, we say, will satisfy our hopes;
Tomorrow comes, and leaves us still more miserable.
What is the flaw, alas, in the care that devours us?
None of us would wish to begin our lives again;
From our first moments we curse the dawn,
And yet we still expect, from the night that comes,
What the most beautiful of days but promises in vain.]

It is in these fragments that English tragedians have thus far excelled; their plays, almost all barbaric, lacking decorum, order, verisimilitude, have these astonishing flashes in the midst of darkness. The style is too swollen, too outrageous, too much copied from Hebrew writing so filled with Asiatic excess; but it must also be acknowledged that the stilts of the figurative style on which the English language is hoisted do elevate the mind, though with an uneven stride.

The first Englishman to compose a well-designed play, elegantly written from one end to the other, is the illustrious Mr. Addison. His *Cato of Utica* is a masterpiece of language and beautiful verse.[8] The role of Cato is, to my mind, far above that of Cornelia in Corneille's *Pompey*,[9] for Cato is great without pomposity, and Cornelia, who is not, moreover, a necessary character, at times verges on the ridiculous. Mr. Addison's Cato seems to me the most noble character to be seen on any stage, but the other characters do not match him, and the work, so well written, is marred by a chilly love affair that infects the play with a deadly slowness.

The habit of introducing love helter-skelter into dramatic works came from Paris to London in about the year 1660, together with our ribbons and wigs. Women, who adorn these performances as they do here, were no longer willing to have dramatists address anything other than love. Addison, that wise man, weakly complaisant and willing to bend the austerity of his character to the customs of the times, spoiled a masterpiece for the sake of pleasing.

Since then, plays have become more conventional, the audience more demanding, the authors more correct and less daring. I have seen some new plays, wise but chilly. It seems that the English have until now been able to produce only uneven beauty. Shakespeare's brilliant monstrosities please a thousand times more than today's elegance. The poetic genius of the English still seems more like a bushy tree planted by nature, branching out at random, growing unevenly and strongly; it dies if you try to alter its nature and prune its branches into the topiary gardens of Marly.[10]

NINETEENTH LETTER

On Comedy

I do not know why the sagacious and intelligent Mr. de Muralt, whose *Letters on the English and the French* we have,[1] restrained himself to criticism of a comedian named Shadwell, when writing about comedy.[2] This author was somewhat scorned in his day; he was not a poet for respectable people. His plays, which the populace enjoyed a few times, were disdained by all the people with good taste, and resembled many of the plays I have seen in France, which draw crowds and disgust readers, and of which it has been said, "All Paris attacks them, and rushes to see them."[3]

Mr. de Muralt ought, it seems, to have discussed an excellent author of the time: this was Mr. Wycherley, who was for a long time the recognized lover of the most illustrious mistress of Charles II.[4] This man, who spent his life in the highest society, knew its vices and foolishness perfectly, and painted them with the steadiest brush and in their truest colors.

He wrote a *Misanthrope*, in which he imitated Molière.[5] All the traits of Wycherley's character are more developed and daring than they are in our misanthrope; but they are also less refined and correct. The English author has repaired the one flaw in Molière's play; this defect is its lack of intrigue and interest. The English play is engaging, and the intrigue is ingeniously devised: it is doubtless too daring for our taste. The hero is a ship's captain, valiant, open, and full of scorn for the human race. He has a wise and sincere friend whom he mistrusts, a mistress who loves him tenderly and at whom he does not deign to look; on the contrary, he has placed his confidence in a false friend who is the least worthy man alive, and he has given his heart to the most flirtatious and unfaithful of women. He assures himself that this woman is a Penelope and this false friend a Cato. He departs to fight the Dutch and leaves all his money, his jewels, indeed all that he has in the world, to this worthy woman, entrusting her to this faithful friend on whom he entirely relies. However, the truly honest man whom he mistrusts embarks with him, and the woman he did not deign to look at disguises herself as a page and accompanies him during the entire campaign without his being aware of her sex.

75

The captain, who has destroyed his vessel during a battle, returns to London, without resources, vessel, or money, accompanied by his page and his friend, recognizing neither the friendship of the one nor the love of the other. He goes directly to his pearl among women, expecting to find his moneybox and her devotion; he finds her married to the scoundrel in whom he confided, but not his money or anything else. Our hero has infinite difficulty in believing that a virtuous woman could behave in this way; but the better to convince him, this honest woman becomes besotted by the page, whom she wishes to seize by force. But since justice must be done, and in a play vice must be punished and virtue rewarded, at the end the captain takes the place of his page, sleeps with his unfaithful lady, cuckolds his treacherous friend, runs his sword through him, takes back his coffer, and marries the page. Please note that the play has been fattened by the introduction of the Countess of Pinchbeck, a litigious old relation of the captain, and the most amusing and comical character ever to appear in a play.

Wycherley also drew from Moliere an equally remarkable and no less daring play—a kind of *School for Wives*.[6] The principal character in the play is an amusing philanderer, the terror of all the husbands in London, who, to make his position more secure, decides to spread the rumor that during his last illness the surgeons felt it necessary to make him a eunuch. Hearing this report, all the men visit him with their wives, and the poor man is embarrassed only by the wealth of choices. He prefers a young country girl, innocent and of lively character, who betrays her husband with a guilelessness that is more effective than all the malice of the most experienced of women. This play is not, if you like, a model of good behavior, but it is in fact a model of wit and comedy.

Sir [John] Vanbrugh wrote even more amusing comedies, although they were less ingenious. This knight was devoted to pleasure and was also a poet and architect; it is said that he wrote as he built, in a somewhat vulgar fashion. It is he who built the famous Blenheim Palace, a heavy and durable monument to our unfortunate Battle of Hochstaedt.[7] If the rooms were as large as the walls are thick, the palace would be comfortable enough.

His epitaph reads, "in hopes that the earth would lie heavily upon him, given how cruelly his buildings weighed it down."[8]

This knight, having made a tour of France before the war of 1701, was put into the Bastille and remained there for some time without having been able to learn what he had done to earn such ministerial distinction. He wrote a comedy while in the Bastille; and what is very strange, to my way of thinking, is that there is in it no criticism of the country that made him suffer this affront.[9]

The Englishman who carried the glory of comedy the farthest was the late Mr. Congreve.[10] He wrote but few plays, but all are excellent in their fashion. The rules of theater are rigorously observed; the plays are full of well-drawn characters; they never subject one to vulgar humor; you will hear the language of decent folk performing scurrilous deeds. This proves that he knew his world well and that he lived in what is called good company. He was weak and almost at the point of death when I met him; he had one fault, which was that he did not sufficiently value his profession as a writer, a profession that made his reputation and his fortune. He spoke to me about his works as if they were trifles, beneath his ability, and told me, in our first conversation, to consider him solely as a gentleman who led a simple life. I told him that if he had had the misfortune to be merely a gentleman like any other I would never have come to visit him, and I was quite shocked by his misdirected vanity.

His plays are the wittiest and most accurate; those of Vanbrugh the most comical; and those of Wycherley the most daring.

One must note that none of these witty men spoke ill of Molière. Only bad English writers have said bad things about this great man. There are poor musicians in Italy who scorn Lully,[11] but someone like Bononcini values his work and does justice to him, just as Mead admires Helvétius and Silva.[12]

England still has good comic poets like Steele and Cibber,[13] an excellent writer of comedy as well as poet to the king, a title that seems ridiculous but which nonetheless is worth a thousand crowns of income as well as handsome privileges. Our great Corneille did not receive so much.

Finally, do not ask me to give details of those English plays of which I am such a hearty partisan, nor to give you a witticism from the Wycherleys and the Congreves; people do not laugh at wit in translation. The only way to understand English comedy is to go to London, stay there for three years, learn English well, and go to the theater every day. I do not much enjoy reading Plautus and Aristophanes.[14] Why? Because I am neither Greek nor Roman. The subtle witticism, the allusions, the relevance of the lines, all are lost on a foreigner.

The same is not true of tragedy; there it is always a matter of great passions and heroic follies, canonized by old misunderstandings of fable or history. Oedipus, Electra belong to the Spanish, the English, and to us, as they did to the Greeks. But good comedy is a speaking image of the follies of a nation, and if you do not know the nation well, you will not be able to judge its portrait.

TWENTIETH LETTER

On Noblemen Who Cultivate Literature

There was a time in France when the arts were cultivated by the mightiest in the state. This was especially true of courtiers, despite the dissipation, the taste for trifles, the passion for intrigue that were the reigning deities of the land.

It seems to me that in the court these days there is a taste for something quite different from letters. Perhaps in a little while thinking will be in fashion again: a king has only to wish for something; the nation becomes anything he wants. In England people commonly do think, and letters there are more honored than they are in France.[1] This advantage is the necessary result of their form of government. In London there are about eight hundred people who have the right to speak publicly and to engage in national affairs; some five or six thousand imagine they have the same honor; all the rest become critics of these people, and anyone may publish whatever he thinks about public matters. Thus, the whole nation is obliged to be informed. The governments of Athens and of Rome are everywhere the subject of conversation. Everyone speaks of Athens and Rome; whatever one's taste, one must read the authors who have written about such things; these studies naturally lead to literature. For the most part, men's minds correspond to their station in life. Why, ordinarily, are our magistrates, lawyers, physicians, and many ecclesiastics, more given to letters, and possessed of better taste and intelligence than men in all other professions? It is because their work demands a cultivated mind, as a merchant must have a talent for business. Not long ago a very young English nobleman on his way home from Italy came to see me in Paris; he had described that place in verse as elegantly written as if it had been composed by Lord Rochester,[2] or Chaulieu, Sarrassin or Chapelle.

The translation I have made of his verses is so far from attaining the strength and the wit of the original that I am obliged most humbly to beg pardon of the author and of those who know English; nevertheless, since I have no other way to make known the verses of Milord . . . ,[3] here they are in my own tongue.[4]

[Volaire's French translation of Hervey:]

Qu'ai-je donc vu dans l'Italie?
Orgueil, astuce et pauvreté,
Grands compliments, peu de bonté,
Et beaucoup de cérémonie;
L'extravagante comedie
Que souvent l'Inquisition
Veut qu'on nomme religion,
Mais qu'ici nous nommons folie.[5]
La nature, en vain bienfaisante,
Veut enrichir ces lieux charmants,
Des prêtres la main désolante
Étouffe ses plus beaux presents.
Les monsignors, soi-disant grands,
Seuls dans leurs palais magnifiques
Y sont d'illustres fainéants,
Sans argent et sans domestiques.
Pour les petits, sans liberté,
Martyrs du joug qui les domine,
Ils ont fait voeu de pauvreté,
Priant Dieu par oisiveté,
Et toujours jeûnant par famine.
Ces beaux lieux, du pape bénis,
Semblent habités par les diables,
Et les habitants misérables
Sont damnés dans le paradis.

One might say that these are the lines of a heretic, but every day we see translations, even bad ones, of Horace and Juvenal, who had the misfortune to be pagans. You know very well that a translator should not be responsible for the sentiments of his author; all that he can do is to pray to God for his conversion, which I will not fail to do for Milord.

[English text of the poem by John Hervey, Baron of Ickworth:[6]

Throughout all Italy besides
What does one find but want and pride,
Farces of superstitious folly,
Decay, distress and melancholy,

The havock of despotick power,
A country rich, its owners poor,
Unpeopled towns, and lands untill'd,
Bodies uncloath'd, and mouths unfilled.
The nobles miserably great
In painted domes and [humble *biffé*] empty state,
Too proud to work, too poor to eat?
No art the meaner sort employ,
They nought improve, nor ought enjoye,
Each clown from misery grows a saint,
He prays from idleness, and fasts from want.[7]]

TWENTY-FIRST LETTER

On the Earl of Rochester and Mr. Waller

Everyone knows the Earl of Rochester by reputation.[1] M. de Saint-Evremond wrote much about him but showed us only the man of pleasure, the philanderer. I would like to have him recognized as a man of genius and as a great poet. Among other works that sparkle with the ardent imagination that belonged only to him are some satires on the same subjects chosen by our own celebrated Despréaux. I know nothing more useful for cultivating good taste than the comparison of great minds that addressed the same materials.

Here is how M. Despréaux argued against human reason in his satire on mankind:

[Depreaux's French text:

Cependant, à le voir, plein de vapeurs légères,
Soi-même se bercer de ses propres chimères,
Lui seul de la nature est la base et l'appui,
Et le dixième ciel ne tourne que pour lui.
De tous les animaux il est ici le maître;
Qui pourrait le nier, poursuis-tu? Moi, peut-être:
Ce maître prétendu, qui leur donne des lois,
Ce roi des animaux, combine a-t-il de rois?]

[English translation of Depreaux's French text:

Yet see him, filled with airy thoughts,
Nursing himself in his own illusions,
He thinks himself the base and support of nature,
And that the highest heavens revolve for him alone.
Of all the animals he is the master;
Who denies this, you ask? Perhaps it is I:
This would-be master who gives them their laws,
This king of the beasts, how many kings has he?[2]]

This is more or less the way the Earl of Rochester expresses himself in his satire on mankind; but the reader must always remind himself that these are free translations of the English poets, and that the constraints of our versification and the delicate conventions of our language cannot convey the impetuous freedom of English style:[3]

[Voltaire's condensed French translation of Rochester:]

> Cet esprit que je hais, cet esprit plein d'erreur,
> Ce n'est pas ma raison, c'est la tienne, docteur;
> C'est ta raison frivole, inquiète, orgueilleuse,
> Des sages animaux rivale dédaigneuse,
> Qui croit entre eux et l'ange occuper le milieu,
> Et pense être ici-bas l'image de son Dieu,
> Vil atome importun, qui croit, doute, dispute,
> Rampe, s'élève, tombe, et nie encor [*sic*] sa chute;
> Qui nous dit: "Je suis libre," en nous montrant ses fers,
> Et dont l'oeil trouble et faux croit percer l'Univers,
> Allez, révérends fous, bienheureux fanatiques,
> Compilez bien l'amas de vos riens scolastiques!
> Pères de visions et d'énigmes sacrés,
> Auteurs du labyrinthe où vous vous égarez,
> Allez obscurément éclaircir vos mystères,
> Et courez dans l'école adorer vos chimeres!
> Il est d'autres erreurs, il est de ces dévots
> Condamnés par eux-même à l'ennui du repos.
> Ce mystique encloîtré, fier de son indolence,
> Tranquille au sein de Dieu, qu'y peut-il faire? Il pense.
> Non, tu ne penses point, miserable, tu dors:
> Inutile à la terre et mis au rang des morts,
> Ton esprit énervé croupit dans la mollesse;
> Réveille-toi, sois homme, et sors de ton ivresse.
> L'homme est né pour agir, et tu prétends penser!

[English translation of the above:

> This spirit I hate, this error-filled spirit,
> Is not my reasoning, it is thine, Doctor;
> It is thy frivolous, uneasy, vainglorious reason,
> Disdainful rival of the wise animals,
> Which believes itself the midpoint between beast and angel,

And thinks it is the image of God in this world.
Vile importunate atom who believes, doubts, disputes,
Crawls, raises itself, falls, and still denies its fall;
Who tells us, "I am free," while displaying its chains,
Whose eye, blurred and dull, thinks it sees the whole world,
Come, holy madmen, happy fanatics!
Heap up the debris of your scholastic trivia!
Progenitors of visions and holy enigmas,
Creators of labyrinths in which you go astray,
Go on, obscurely enlighten your mysteries,
Run to the Schools to worship your inventions!
Like other wanderers, those pious worshippers
Self-imprisoned in boring idleness,
This cloistered mystic, proud of his indolence,
Tranquil in God's bosom, what does he there? He thinks.
No, wretch, thou dost not think, thou sleepest:
Of no use to the world, listed among the dead,
Thy weak-willed spirit crouches languidly.
Awake! be man, and leave thy drunkenness,
Man is born to act, yet dost thou claim to think!]

Whether these thoughts be true or false, it is certain that they are expressed with the energy that defines a poet.

I will refrain from examining this matter as a philosopher and from abandoning the paintbrush for the compasses. My only aim in this letter is to let you know the genius of the English poets, and I will continue in this vein.

In France we have heard much about this famous Waller.[4] Messieurs de La Fontaine, Saint-Evremond, and Bayle praised him; but most people know only his name. In London his reputation was much like that of Voiture[5] in Paris, and I think he deserved it much more. Voiture appeared in the days when we were just emerging from barbarism, when we were still unlettered. Writers sought to have wit and did not yet have it; they looked for turns of phrase rather than ideas false diamonds are more easily found than precious stones. Voiture, endowed with easy and frivolous wit, was the first in French literature to shine this way; had he appeared after the great men who made the century of Louis XIV so illustrious, he would either have been unknown, or he would have been disdained, or he would have corrected his style. M. Despréaux praises him, but only in his early satires, while his taste was still unformed; he was young and at an age when one judges men by their reputation and not by their worth. Moreover, Despréaux is often unjust in his praise and his censure. He praised Segrais,[6] whom no one reads; he insulted Quinault,[7] whom everyone knows by heart, and he said nothing about La Fontaine.[8] Waller, better than Voiture, was still not perfect; his courtly works are full of grace, but carelessness weakens and misjudgments often disfigure them. In his day the English had not yet learned to write correctly. His serious works are full of a vigor that one would not have expected upon reading the weaker ones. He wrote a funeral eulogy for Cromwell, which, despite its defects, is accepted as a masterpiece; to understand this work, one must know that Cromwell died during an extraordinary tempest.[9]

The piece begins thus:

[Voltaire's French translation of Waller:]

> Il n'est plus, c'en est fait, soumettons nous au sort,
> Le ciel a signalé ce jour par des tempêtes,
> Et la voix du tonnerre éclatant sur nos têtes
> Vient d'annoncer sa mort.
> Par ses derniers soupirs il ébranle cet île;
> Cet île que son bras fit trembler tant de fois,
> Quand dans le cours de ses exploits,
> Il brisoit la tête des Rois,
> Et soumettoit un peuple à son joug seul docile.
> "Mer tu t'en es troublé; O mer tes flots émus
> Semblent dire en grondant aux plus lointains rivages
> Que l'effroi de la terre et ton maitre n'est plus.
> Tel au ciel autrefois s'envola Romulus,
> Tel il quitta la terre, au milieu des orages,
> Tel d'un peuple guerrier il reçut les homages;
> Obéi dans sa vie, à sa mort adoré,
> Son palais fut un temple," &c.

[Voltaire's English translation of the above:]

> He is no more, it is finished; let us submit to fate:
> The heavens have marked this day by tempest,
> And thunder, breaking over our heads,
>   Has just announced his death.
> With his last sighs he shakes the isle,
> This isle that his arm so often shook

> When, by his exploits,
> He broke the heads of kings
> And tamed a people docile under his yoke alone.
> Sea, thou are troubled; O sea, thy tossing waves,
> Seem to say, groaning on most distant shores,
> That the terror of the earth, your master, has gone.
> Thus did Romulus once mount the sky,
> Thus he left the earth in the midst of storms,
> Thus he received the homage of a warrior folk;
> Obeyed in his life, adored in death,
> His palace became a temple, etc.[10]

[Original lines by Waller, which appear in the 1733 translation:]

> We must resign! Heav'n his great soul does claim
> In storms as loud as his immortal Fame:
> His dying Groans, his last Breath shakes our Isle,
> And Trees uncut fall for his fun'ral Pile:
> About his Palace their broad Roots are toss't
> Into the Air: so *Romulus* was lost!
> New *Rome* in such a Tempest miss'd her King,
> And from obeying fell to worshipping:
> On *Aetna*'s Top thus *Hercules* lay dead,
> With ruin'd Oaks and Pines about him spread.
> Nature herself took Notice of his Death,
> And, sighing, swell'd the Sea with such a Breath,
> That to remotest Shores the Billows roll'd,
> Th' approaching Fate of his great Ruler told.

It was with reference to this eulogy of Cromwell that Waller made the following remark to Charles II, which is reported in Bayle's dictionary. The king, to whom Waller had just presented a piece larded with praise—as poets do for kings—reproached Waller for having written a better one for Cromwell. Waller replied, "Sire, we poets are more successful authors of fiction than of truth." This reply was not as sincere as that of the Dutch ambassador, who, when the same king complained that he was less well thought of than Cromwell, replied, "Ah! Sire, this Cromwell was something quite different."

My aim is not to write a commentary on the character of Waller, or of anyone else; after their death I value persons only by their works; all the rest disappears. I would say only that Waller, born to courtly life[11] with sixty thousand pounds of income, never allowed stupid pride or laziness to lead him to neglect his talent. The Earls of Dorset and of Roscommon, the two Lords Buckingham, My Lord Halifax,[12] and so many others did not imagine they lowered themselves by becoming great poets and illustrious writers. They are more honored for their works than for their names. They cultivated letters as if their fortunes depended on them; moreover, they made the arts respectable in the eyes of the common people who need, in all matters, to be guided by the great, although noblemen are imitated less in England than they are elsewhere in the world.

Twenty-Second Letter

On Mr. Pope, and Some Other Famous Poets

I wanted to tell you about Mr. Prior, one of the most agreeable poets of England, whom you saw in Paris in 1712 as Envoy Extraordinary and Plenipontentiary.[1] I planned also to give you a few thoughts on the poems of Lord Roscommon, Lord Dorset, etc., but I sense that this would require a great thick book, and that after much difficulty I would only have given you a most imperfect understanding of all these works. Poetry is a kind of music; one must hear it in order to judge it. When I translate a few bits of these foreign poems for you I indicate, imperfectly, their melody, but I cannot express the sonority of the music.

There is in particular one English poem that I would despair of making known to you: called *Hudibras*, it ridicules the civil war and the sect of the Puritans.[2] It is a combination of *Don Quixote* and our *Menippean Satire*;[3] it is, of all the books I have ever read, the wittiest, but it is also the most untranslatable. Who would believe that a book that pounces upon all the folly of mankind, and that has more ideas than words, would not permit of translation? The reason is that almost all of it refers to specific incidents: the largest part of the ridicule is directed at theologians whom few members of worldly society understand. At every turn one would need a commentary, and a joke explained is a joke that has failed; anyone who annotates a witticism is a fool.

This is why no one in France will ever understand the books of the ingenious Doctor Swift, who is called the Rabelais of England.[4] Like Rabelais, he has the honor of being a cleric, and, like Rabelais, mocks everything; but it is a great mistake, I believe, to identify him thus. Rabelais, in his extravagant and incomprehensible book, radiated extraordinary gaiety and even greater impertinence: he lavished on us erudition, excrement, and tediousness; a good two-page story is worth more than volumes of stupidity. Only a few people, with bizarre tastes, pride themselves on understanding and enjoying all this stuff; the rest of the nation laughs at Rabelais' jokes and scoffs at the book. Readers consider him the master of buffoonery; they are annoyed that a man who had so much wit should have used it so badly; he was a drunken philosopher who only wrote while he was drunk.

Mr. Swift is Rabelais at his best, living in better company; it is true that he has not the gaiety of the latter, but he has all the elegance, the reason, the discrimination, the good taste lacking in our *curé* of Meudon. His poetry demonstrates a remarkable and almost inimitable style; he has the gift of good humor in verse as in prose; but to understand him properly one must make a little visit to his country.

You may more easily form an impression of Mr. Pope;[5] he is, I believe, the most elegant, the most correct, and, what is still more, the most musical poet that England has ever had. He transmuted the harsh blasts of the English trumpet into the soft notes of the flute. He can be translated because his writing is extremely clear, and his subjects are, for the most part, general and common to every nation.

France will soon know his *Essay on Criticism*, thanks to the verse translation that M. the Abbé de Resnel is preparing.[6]

Here is a part of his poem called *The Rape of the Lock*,[7] which I have recently translated with my usual freedom; for once again, I know nothing worse than translating a poem word for word:

[Voltaire's French translation:]

> Umbriel à l'instant, vieux gnome rechigné,
> Va, d'une aile pesante et d'un air refrogné,
> Chercher, en murmurant, la caverne profonde
> Où, loin des doux rayons que répand l'oeil du monde,
> La déesse aux vapeurs a choisi son séjour.
> Les tristes aquilons y sifflent à l'entour,
> Et le souffle malsain de leur aride haleine
> Y port aux environs la fièvre et la migraine.
> Sur un riche sofa, derrière un paravent,
> Loin des flambeaux, du bruit, des parleurs et du vent,
> La quinteuse déese incessamment repose,
> Le coeur gros de chagrins, sans en avoir la cause,
> N'ayant pensé jamais, l'esprit toujours troublé
> L'oeil chargé, le teint pale, et l'hypocondre enflé.
> La médisante Envie est assise auprès d'elle,
> Vieux spectre feminine, décrépite pucelle,
> Avec un air dévot déchirant son prochain,
> Et chansonnant les gens l'Evangile à la main.
> Sur un lit plein de fleurs négligemment penchée,

Une jeune beauté non loin d'elle est couchée:
C'est l'Affectation, qui grasseye en parlant,
Écoute sans entendre, et lorgne en regardant,
Qui rougit sans pudeur, et rit de tout sans joie,
De cent maux différents pretend qu'elle est la proie,
Et pleine de santé sous le rouge et le fard,
Se plaint avec mollesse, et se pâme avec art.

[This is the text of Alexander Pope's original:[8]]

Umbriel, a dusky, melancholy Sprite
As ever sullied the fair Face of Light,
Down to the central Earth, his proper Scene,
Repairs to search the gloomy Cave of *Spleen*.
Swift on his sooty Pinions flits the *Gnome*,
And in a Vapour reach'd the dismal Dome.
No cheerful Breeze this sullen Region knows,
The dreaded East is all the Wind that blows.
Here, in a Grotto, shelter'd close from Air
And screen'd in Shades from Day's detested Glare,
She sighs for ever on her pensive Bed.
Pain at her Side, and *Megrim* at her Head,
Two Handmaids wait the Throne: Alike in Place,
But diff'ring far in Figure and in Face,
Here stood *Ill-nature* like an ancient Maid,
Her wrinkled Form in black and white array'd;
With Store of Prayers of Mornings, Nights, and Noons,
Her Hand is fill'd; her Bosom with Lampoons.
There *Affectation*, with a sickly Mein,
Shows in her Cheek the roses of eighteen,
Practics'd to lisp, and hang the Head aside,
Faints into Airs, and languishes with Pride;
On the Rich Quilt sinks with becoming Woe,
Wrapt in a Gown, for Sickness and for Show.

If you read this piece in the original instead of in this feeble translation you might compare it with the description of Apathy in *Le
Lutrin*.[9]

Here, as directly as possible, is what I can say about the English
poets. I have told you a little about their philosophers. As for good
historians, I do not yet know any; a Frenchman was needed to write

their history. Perhaps the English genius, which is either cold or stormy, has not yet mastered the direct eloquence and the noble and simple style of the historian; perhaps also the spirit of party, which distorts one's vision, has invalidated all their historians. One half of the nation is always the enemy of the other. I have met some who assured me that Lord Marlborough was a poltroon, and that M. Pope was a fool, as in France some Jesuits find Pascal insignificant, and some Jansenists say that Father Bourdaloue was only a chatterer.[10] Mary Stuart was a saintly heroine for the Jacobites;[11] for the others, she was a debauched woman, an adulteress, and a murderer; thus in England there are only arguments and no history. There is at present a certain Mr. Gordon,[12] an excellent translator of Tacitus, who would be capable of writing the history of his country, but Mr. Rapin de Thoiras[13] has anticipated him. Indeed, it seems to me that the English do not have as good historians as we do; they have no true tragedies; they have charming comedies, some admirable poetic works, and philosophers who should be the teachers of the human race.

The English have profited from works in our language; having lent to them we should in turn borrow from them. We, the English and ourselves, have appeared only after the Italians, who have been in all things our masters and whom we have surpassed in some respects. I do not know which of the three countries deserves the greatest honor; but happy the one who knows how to recognize the merits of each!

TWENTY-THIRD LETTER

On the Esteem Due to Men of Letters

Neither in England nor in any other country in the world does one find institutions that encourage the fine arts like those of France. There are universities almost everywhere, but only in France does one find these useful institutions that support astronomy and all the branches of mathematics, medicine, research into Antiquity, painting, sculpture, and architecture.[1] Louis XIV was immortalized by all these foundations, and this immortality cost him barely two hundred thousand francs a year.

I admit that I am astonished that the Parliament of England, which announced a prize of twenty thousand guineas to the person who should do the impossible and discover how to determine longitude, has never sought to imitate Louis XIV in his generosity to the arts.[2]

It is true that in England merit is rewarded in ways that do greater honor to the nation; such is the respect that this people has for talent that a man of merit is assured of a fortune. In France, M. Addison[3] would have belonged to an academy, and, thanks to some noblewoman, might have received a pension of twelve hundred pounds; or rather he might have been attacked on the pretext that in his tragedy *Cato* he had insulted the porter of a distinguished man; in England he was Secretary of State. M. Newton was master of the Royal Mint;[4] M. Congreve[5] had an important public office; M. Prior was an envoy plenipotentiary. Doctor Swift is a Dean in Ireland[6] and is held in more esteem than the bishop. If M. Pope's [religion prevents him from holding public office, it has not prevented his translation of Homer from earning him two hundred thousand [francs].[7] In France I saw the author of *Rhadamiste* close to starving for many years;[8] and the son of one of the greatest men that France ever had, who was beginning to walk in his father's footsteps, would have been reduced to poverty had it not been for M. Fagon.[9] What chiefly encourages the arts in England is the esteem they receive: the portrait of the Prime Minister hangs over the mantelpiece in his office, but I have seen M. Pope's portrait in twenty houses.[10]

M. Newton[11] was honored in his lifetime and after his death as he deserved to be. The chief men of the nation vied for the honor of carrying the pall in his funeral procession. Enter Westminster [Abbey]: it is not the tombs of the kings that one admires, but the monuments that a grateful nation has erected to those great men who contributed to its glory. There you will see their statues, as in Athens one saw the statues of Sophocles and Plato, and I am sure that the mere sight of these glorious monuments has animated more than one soul and shaped more than one great man.

Some have reproached the English for having gone too far in honoring merit alone and censoriously point out that the famous comedienne Mlle. Oldfield[12] was buried with almost the same honors as those accorded to M. Newton. They have claimed that the memory of this actress was thus honored in order to rebuke us for the barbarous and cowardly injustice of throwing the body of Mlle. Lecouvreur[13] into the gutter

But I can assure you that in preparing the funeral for Mlle. Oldfield, who was buried in their equivalent of the church of Saint Denis, the English were expressing their own taste. They are far from considering infamous the art of Sophocles and Euripides, nor do they ostracize those who devote themselves to presenting on stage works in which the nation takes great pride.

In the time of Charles I and at the beginning of the civil wars started by those rigorous fanatics who at last became victims themselves, many attacked theatrical performances, especially because Charles I and his wife, daughter of our Henry the Great,[14] much admired them.

One doctor Prynne,[15] scrupulous in the extreme, who would have thought himself damned had he worn a cassock rather than a short coat, and who would have wished that half of mankind might massacre the other half for the glory of God and the propagation of the faith, took it upon himself to write a very bad book against the fairly good comedies that were most innocently acted in the presence of the king and the queen. He cited as authorities rabbis and some passages written by Saint Bonaventure to prove that Sophocles' *Oedipus*[16] was the work of the Evil One, that Terence was excommunicated *ipso facto*; and he added that Brutus, a strict Jansenist, had doubtless assassinated Caesar, a high priest, only because Caesar had written a tragedy called *Oedipus*. Indeed, he concluded that all who are present at a play are excommunicants who have renounced their chrism and their baptism. This was an insult to the king and the whole royal family. In those days the English respected Charles I; at that time they refused to permit talk of excommunicating the king whose head they later chopped off. M. Prynne was brought before the Court of Star Chamber, condemned to see his fine book burned by the executioner, and to have his ears cut off; you can read about his trial in the public registers.

In Italy one must be careful to avoid condemning the Opera and excommunicating Signor Senesino or Signora Cuzzoni.[17] As for me, I dare to wish that in France one might suppress all those bad books that attack our theaters; for once the Italians and the English learn that we stigmatize as disgraceful an art in which we excel, that we condemn as impious a play performed for the clergy and in convents, that we dishonor the entertainment in which Louis XIV and Louis XV took parts, that we call devilish those works overseen by the most stringent magistrates and performed in the presence of a virtuous queen—when, I say, foreigners learn of this insolence, this lack of respect for royal authority, this gothic barbarity that some dare call Christian severity, what might they think of our nation, and how could they understand, either that our laws would countenance so infamous an art, or that we dare to call infamous an art authorized by law, rewarded by sovereigns, cultivated by great men, and admired by other nations; and, more, that, in the same bookshop, Father Le Brun's[18] condemnation of our plays is found side by side with the immortal works of Racine, Corneille, Molière, etc.?

TWENTY-FOURTH LETTER

On the Academies

The English had an Academy of Sciences long before we did, but it is not as well regulated as is ours, and this perhaps only because it is the older, for, had it been formed after the Academy of Paris, it would have adopted some of its wise regulations, and improved others.

The Royal Society of London[1] lacks the two elements most necessary to men—rewards and rules. A geometer, a chemist in Paris is assured of a small fortune if he is a member of the Academy; on the other hand, a member of the Royal Society in London must pay something. In England anyone who says, "I love the arts," and wants to be a member of the Society becomes one instantly. But in France, to be a member and pensioner of the Academy it is not enough to be a lover of knowledge; one must be learned and contend for admission against rivals who are all the more imposing because they are driven by the desire for glory, by self-interest, even by the difficulty of the process, and by that rigidity of spirit that results from the relentless study of mathematics.[2]

Our Academy of Sciences is wisely limited to the study of nature, and, to be sure, that is a field large enough to occupy fifty or sixty people. The one in London mixes literature and science without discrimination. It seems to me that it is better to have an academy devoted to literature, so that matters are not jumbled together, and one does not see a dissertation on Roman hair styles next to a hundred new formulae for curves.

Since the London Society offers little order and no support, and since the one in Paris is built on a very different foundation, it is not surprising that the Transactions of our academy should be superior to theirs; well-disciplined and well-paid soldiers must at length overcome volunteers. It is true that the Royal Society had its Newton, but it did not produce him; indeed, there were few members who understood him; a genius like M. Newton belonged to all the Academies of Europe, because all had much to learn from him.[3]

In the last years of the reign of Queen Anne, the famous Doctor Swift presented a project to create an academy that would define the language, following the example of the French Academy. The project was supported by the Earl of Oxford, the Lord Treasurer of England, and even more by Viscount Bolingbroke, Secretary of State, who had the gift of speaking extemporaneously in Parliament with as much purity of language as Swift demonstrated in his writing, and who would have been the protector and ornament of this academy.[4] Its members were to be those men whose works will endure as long as the English language: Doctor Swift; M. Prior, whom we have seen as special envoy and who in England enjoys the same reputation that La Fontaine has with us; M. Pope, the Boileau of England; M. Congreve, whom one might call their Molière; several others whose names I now forget would all have made this company flourish in its infancy. But the Queen died suddenly; the Whigs took it into their heads to hang the protectors of the academy, which, as you may imagine, was a mortal blow to literature. The members of this company would have had a great advantage over those who first formed the French Academy; for Swift, Prior, Congreve, Dryden, Pope, Addison, etc., had established the English language in their writing, whereas Chapelain, Colletet, Cassaigne, Faret, Perrin, Cotin, your first Academicians, were the laughingstock of your nation, and their names have become so contemptible that if some decent author had the misfortune to be called Chapelain or Cotin, he would be obliged to change his name.[5] Above all, the English Academy ought to have set for itself tasks that were different from ours. One day an English wit asked me for the Transactions of the French Academy. "It does not produce Transactions," I answered him, "but it has published sixty or eighty volumes of compliments." He skimmed one or two; he could not manage to understand their style, although he understood all our good authors quite well. "All that I see here in these fine speeches," said he to me, "is that the new member asserts that his predecessor was a great man, that Cardinal Richelieu was a very great man, that Chancellor Séguier was a fairly great man, that Louis XIV was more than great; and that the director answers in kind and adds that the new member might well be another great man, and that as far as he, the director, was concerned, he too shares in this esteem."[6]

It is easy to see why such flawed discourses have brought so little honor to the body: "It was the vice of the era, not of the man."[7] Custom imperceptibly required each academician to repeat these eulogies when he was admitted; boring the public became a kind of law.[8] If one seeks then to learn why the greatest geniuses who were admitted to this body sometimes wrote the worst speeches, the reason is easy to find: it is that they wanted to shine; they wanted to treat a worn-out topic in a new way; the need to speak, the awkwardness of having nothing to say, and the desire of being witty are three things capable of making the greatest man seem foolish. Unable to find new ideas, they sought new turns of phrase and spoke without thinking, like those who chew with empty mouths, and pretend to be eating while they are starving.

Although there is a law in the French Academy that these discourses must be published, since only by them is the Academy known, there should be a law that they not be published.

The Academy of literature chose a wiser and more useful purpose: to give to the public a collection of Transactions containing investigations and interesting reviews. These Transactions are already valued by foreigners; one would only wish that some matters were treated more thoroughly and others not treated at all. We might well have done without a discussion of the advantages of the right hand over the left hand, and other investigations with less foolish titles and equally frivolous content.[9]

The Academy of sciences, engaged in more difficult and more patently useful investigations, is devoted to the knowledge of nature and the perfection of the arts. One may well believe that such deep and systematic studies, such precise calculations, such refined discoveries, such expansive projects, will at length produce something that will benefit the universe.

Until now, as we have already seen, it is in the most primitive centuries that the most useful discoveries have been made; it seems that the lot of the most enlightened centuries and the most learned of associations is but to explicate the inventions of the ignorant. Thanks to the long debates of M. Huygens and M. Renau,[10] we now can determine the best angular relationship between the tiller and the keel; but Christopher Columbus discovered America without any knowledge of this angle.

I am very far from inferring from this fact that we must keep to blind habit, but it would be fortunate if geometers and students of physics brought together, as much as possible, the practical and the theoretical. Must it be that those things that do most honor to the human spirit are so often the least useful? A man who knows the four rules of arithmetic and has some good sense becomes a great merchant, a Jacques Coeur, a Delmet, a Bernard,[11] whereas a poor arithmetician spends his life searching for astonishing relationships and properties of numbers that are useless and will not teach him anything about trade. All the arts are more or less in this condition.

There is a point beyond which research satisfies only curiosity; those ingenious and useless truths resemble stars that are too far from us to give us any light.

As for the French Academy, what service would it not render to literature, to our language, and to the nation if, instead of publishing compliments every year, it printed the great works of the reign of Louis XIV, purged of all the mistakes in language that have slipped into them? Corneille and Molière are full of them; they swarm in La Fontaine; those that could not be corrected would at least be indicated. The Europe that reads these authors would learn our language reliably; its purity would be fixed forever; excellent French books, carefully printed at the king's expense, would be one of the most glorious monuments of the nation. I have heard that M. Despréaux had proposed this once before, and that the idea was taken up again by a man whose intelligence, wisdom, and good judgment are well known,[12] but it suffered the fate of many other useful projects: to be approved and neglected.

TWENTY-FIFTH LETTER

On Mr. Pascal's Pensées

I send you the critical notes on Pascal's *Pensées* that I made a long time ago.[1] Pray do not compare me with Hezekiah, who wanted to burn all of Solomon's books.[2] I respect Pascal's genius and eloquence, but the more I respect them, the more I am persuaded that he himself would have corrected many of those *Pensées* that he wrote down haphazardly, intending to examine them later; and it is while I am admiring his genius that I challenge some of his ideas.

It seems to me on the whole that the spirit in which M. Pascal wrote these *Pensées* was to show man in an odious light. He is determined to paint us all as wicked and miserable. He attacks human nature much as he attacked the Jesuits: he imputes to human nature that which is true only for some men; he eloquently insults the human race. I dare to take humanity's part against this sublime misanthrope. I dare to affirm that we are neither so wicked nor so miserable as he claims. More, I am quite persuaded that if, in the book that he intended to write, he had followed the plan that appears in the *Pensées*, he would have written a book full of eloquent illogicalities and admirably deduced inaccuracies. I even believe that all those books that have recently been made to support Christianity are more capable of offending than of edifying. Do those authors pretend to know more than Jesus Christ and the apostles? That is like trying to support an oak with a fence of reeds; one can clear away those useless reeds with no risk of harming the tree.

I have carefully chosen some of Pascal's thoughts; I put my responses below them. It is for you to decide whether I am wrong or right.

I. The grandeur and the misery of man are so visible that true religion must necessarily teach us that there is in him some great principle of grandeur, and at the same time some great principle of misery. For true religion must know our nature in depth, which is to say that it must know about all its greatness and all its misery, and the reasons for each of them. Further, true religion must explain for us these astonishing contradictions.

This kind of reasoning seems false and dangerous, for the fables of Prometheus and Pandora, Plato's androgynous figures, and the dogmas of the Siamese account for these apparent contradictions equally well. Christianity will not be less true if one refrains from drawing such specious conclusions, which serve only to advertise one's wit.

Christianity teaches only simplicity, forbearance, charity: reduce it to metaphysics and it becomes a source of error.

II. Examine this question in all the world's religions, and see whether any other than Christianity can explain it satisfactorily.

Might it be the one that the philosophers taught, which offers as its sole good that good that is within us? Is that true virtue? Have they found the cure for our ills? Does one cure the arrogance of man by making him the equal of God? And those who compare us to the beasts, and who offer earthly pleasure for our highest good, have they provided a remedy for our lust?

The philosophers did not teach religion; it is not their philosophy that must be challenged. No philosopher ever claimed to be inspired by God, for then he would have ceased to be a philosopher and have become a prophet. The issue is not whether Jesus Christ is greater than Aristotle; it is to demonstrate that the religion of Jesus Christ is the true one, and that those of Mohammed, the pagans, and all the others, are false.

III. And nevertheless, absent this most incomprehensible mystery, we are incomprehensible to ourselves. The tangled nature of our condition derives its twists and turns in the abyss of original sin, so that man without this mystery is more incomprehensible than the mystery is itself incomprehensible to man.

Is *Absent this incomprehensible mystery man is incomprehensible* a reasoned statement? Why the desire to go beyond what Scripture says? Is there not some arrogance in believing that Scripture requires some support, and that philosophical ideas can provide it?

How would M. Pascal have replied to a man who might have said to him: "I know that the mystery of original sin is a matter of my faith and not of my reason. I perfectly understand what man is, without added mysteries. I see that he comes into the world like other animals; that a mother's birth-pangs are worse if she is frail; that sometimes women and female animals die in childbirth; that

there are sometimes misformed children who live deprived of one
or more of the senses, or without the ability to think; that those
whose nature is best developed are those that have the liveliest
emotions; that self-esteem is the same in all men, and is as necessary to them as the five senses; that this self-esteem was given to us
by God that we might preserve ourselves, and that He has given us
religion to control this self-esteem; that our ideas are correct or
meaningless, murky or clear to the degree that our organs are more
or less strong, more or less acute, and to the extent that we have
stronger or weaker emotions; that we depend completely on the air
that surrounds us, the food that we eat, and that in all of this there
is nothing contradictory. Man is not a puzzle, as you imagine in
order to have the pleasure of unriddling it. Man seems to be in his
proper place in nature, superior to the animals that he resembles in
body; inferior to other beings that he no doubt resembles by his
ability to think. He is like all that we see, a mixture of bad and good,
of pleasure and pain. He has received emotions to make him act,
and reason by which to govern his actions. If man were perfect, he
would be God; these imagined contrarieties, which you call *contradictions*, are the necessary elements that make up man, who is what
he should be.

   IV. Let us take notice of our acts; let us observe ourselves and see
   whether we do not find living examples of these two natures.

   Could so many contradictions appear in a simple being?

   This double nature of man is so apparent that some have thought
   we have two souls, because a simple subject seems to them incapable
   of such striking and sudden changes, of unbounded presumption and
   a terrible despondency of the heart.

Our different desires are not contradictions in nature, and man is
not a simple being. He is made up of an innumerable number of
organs. If one of these organs is the least bit changed, it must
change all the impressions of his brain, and the animal must then
have new thoughts and new desires. It is very true that we are at
times overcome with sorrow, and at times swollen with pride, and
this must be so when we find ourselves in different situations. An
animal caressed and nourished by its master, and another whose
throat is cut slowly and neatly in order to dissect it, are subject to
very different emotions; we are the same, and the differences within us so little contradict one another that it would be contradictory
if they did not exist.

The fools who have said that we have two souls could as well have said, for the same reason, that we have thirty or forty, for a man in the heat of passion often has thirty or forty different ideas about the same matter, and must necessarily have them as different aspects of the matter present themselves.

This so-called *doubleness* of man is as absurd an idea as it is metaphysical. I could as well say that the dog that bites and caresses has a double nature; that so does the hen that takes such care of her chicks and then abandons them so completely as not to recognize them; that a mirror that shows different objects at the same time is doubled; that the tree that is now leafy, now bare, is doubled. I admit that man is incomprehensible, but so is all of nature, and there are no more apparent contradictions in man than there in all the rest of the world.

> V. Not to wager that God exists is to wager that he does not exist. Which wager will you take? Let us weigh the gain and loss that come with adopting the belief that God exists. If you win, you win all; if you lose, you lose nothing. Wager that He exists, then, without hesitation.—Yes, I must wager; but perhaps I wager too much.—Let us see: since there is equal risk of winning and losing, even if you might win but two lives in exchange for one, you could still win.

Clearly it is false to say, "Not to wager that God exists is to wager that He does not exist," for someone who doubts and wishes to learn is clearly not wagering one way or the other.

Moreover, this entry seems a trifle indecent and childish; this idea of a wager, of loss and gain, ill befits the seriousness of the subject.

And more, my desire to believe a thing is not a proof that this thing exists. I will give you, you might say, the whole world, if I believe you are right. I hope then, with all my heart, that you are right, but until you have proved this, I cannot believe you.

Begin, one might say to M. Pascal, by convincing my reason. I would benefit, no doubt, if there were a god; but if in your doctrine God has come but for so few people, if the number of the elect is frighteningly small, if I can do nothing for myself, tell me, pray, how I should benefit by believing you? Would I not do better to be persuaded of the contrary? How dare you show me infinite happiness to which only one man in a million has the right to aspire? If you wish to convince me, do so differently, and do not at times talk of games of chance, of wagers, of heads and tails, and at other times frighten me by strewing thorns in the path that I wish to take, and must. Your reasoning would but create atheists, if the voice of nature did not cry out that there is a god with as much strength as these subtleties have weakness.

VI. Seeing the blindness and the misery of man, and those astonishing contrarieties that his nature reveals, and seeing all of nature dumb and man without light, abandoned to himself and as if lost in this little corner of the universe, not knowing who put him there, what he was put there to do, what he will become when he dies, I become terrified like a man who has been taken in his sleep to a dreadful desert island, and who awakens not knowing where he is[3] and having no way to escape; and seeing all that I wonder how one could fail to despair in such a miserable condition.

While reading this reflection, I receive a letter from one of my friends who lives in a far distant country. Here is what he writes: "I am here as you left me, neither happier nor sadder, neither richer nor poorer, enjoying perfect health, having everything that makes life pleasant, without love, avarice, ambition, and envy; and as long as these conditions continue, I shall dare to call myself a happy man."

There are many men as happy as he. It is with men as it is with animals. This dog sleeps and eats with its mistress; that one turns a spit and is just as content; another goes mad and is killed. As for me, when I look at Paris or London, I see no reason whatever to feel the despair that M. Pascal describes. I see a city that does not in the least resemble a desert island but is inhabited, opulent, well ordered, where men are as happy as human nature will permit. What wise man would be ready to hang himself because he does not know how to see God face to face, and because his reason cannot untangle the mystery of the Trinity? One might as well despair because one does not have four feet and two wings.

Why make us terrified of our own nature? Our life is not as miserable as some would have us think. To look at the universe as a prison cell, and all men as criminals who will be executed, is the belief of a fanatic. To believe that the world is a place of delights in which one will have only pleasure is the daydream of a sybarite. To believe that the earth, men, and animals are what Providence intended them to be, is, I think, to be a wise man.

VII. (The Jews believe) that God will not forever leave the other nations in darkness; that a redeemer will come for all; that they are in the world to proclaim his coming; that they were created precisely to be the heralds of this great coming and to call all the nations to unite with them in awaiting this redeemer.

The Jews have always expected a redeemer, but their redeemer is for them, not for us. They await a Messiah who will make the Jews masters of the Christians, and we hope that the Messiah will one day unite Jews and Christians; in this respect they believe exactly the opposite of what we believe.

VIII. The law by which this people is governed is the oldest law of the world as well as the most perfect, and the only one that a State has obeyed without interruption. This is what Philo the Jew shows in various places, as does Josephus in *Against Apion*, where he admirably shows that it is so old that the very word *law* was unknown to antiquity for more than a thousand years after it was instituted, so that Homer, who writes of so many nations, never used the word. And it is easy to judge the perfection of this law simply by reading it, wherein one sees that it has provided for so many circumstances with such wisdom, equity, and judgment that the most ancient Greek and Roman legislators, having some knowledge of it, borrowed its central precepts: this is evident in those laws that they called *The Law of the Twelve Tables* and in other proofs that Josephus presents.

It is quite untrue that the law of the Jews is the oldest of laws, since before [the days of] Moses, their legislator, they lived in Egypt, the country the most famous in all the world for its wise laws.

It is quite untrue that the word "law" was not known until after Homer's day: he speaks of the laws of Minos; the word "law" is found in Hesiod; and even if the word "law" were not found either in Hesiod or in Homer,[4] that would prove nothing. There were kings and judges, therefore there were laws.

It is also very untrue that the Greeks and the Romans took their laws from the Jews; this could not have happened at the beginning of their republics, for at that time they could not have been acquainted with the Jews; nor could it have happened in the era of their greatness, for then they held these barbarians in a contempt known to all the world.

IX. This people is also remarkable for their loyalty. They keep lovingly and faithfully the book in which Moses declares that they have always been unfaithful to God; and that he knows they will become yet more so after his death; but that he calls heaven and earth as witnesses against them that he has warned them sufficiently; that at last God, angry with them, will scatter them among all the people of the earth; that as they have angered Him by worshipping gods that were not their gods, so will he anger them by calling on a people that was not His own people. And yet this book that insults them in so many ways is one that they cling to at the risk of their lives. Such loyalty has no counterpart in the world nor its root in nature.

There are examples of such loyalty everywhere, and it has its root in nature alone. The pride of each Jew is invested in the belief that it is not his detestable behavior, his ignorance of the arts, his coarseness that has condemned him, but that it is God's wrath that punishes him. He believes with some satisfaction that only miracles could defeat him, and his nation, which God chastises, is His beloved.

Let a preacher mount the pulpit and say to the French: *"You are miserable creatures who have neither courage nor manners; you were beaten at Hochstaedt and at Ramillies[5] because you did not know how to defend yourselves"*: he would be stoned. But were he to say: *"You are Catholics beloved by God; your terrible sins irritated the Eternal, who gave you up to the heretics at Hochstaedt and at Ramillies; but when you returned to the Lord, he blessed your courage at Denain"*: these words would make him beloved by the congregation.

X. If there is a God, we must love only Him and not his creatures.

We must most tenderly love creatures; we must love our nation, our wife, our father, our children; and it is so necessary to love them that God makes us love them despite ourselves. To believe otherwise serves only to produce uncouth logicians.

XI. We are born wicked, for each person cares only for himself. This is against all order. We must care for all. And that inclination toward oneself is the beginning of all disorder in war, in government, in economy, etc.

This is in accord with all order. It is as impossible for a society to be formed and to persist without self-esteem as it is to create children without desire, to think of feeding oneself without appetite, etc. It is self-esteem that allows us to love others; it is by our common needs that we are useful to the human race; this is the foundation of all commerce; it is the unbreakable bond between men. Without this not one art would have been invented, nor a society of ten people formed; it is this self-esteem, which each animal received from nature, that warns us to respect others. Law controls this love of self, and religion perfects it. It is certainly true that God could have made creatures that care solely for the good of others. In this case, merchants would have gone to the Indies out of charity, and the mason would cut stones to please his neighbor. But God made things differently. Let us not condemn the instinct that He gives us, and let us use it as He commands.

XII. (The hidden meaning of the prophecies) could not induce error, and there was but one nation so carnal as to misunderstand it.

For when blessings are abundantly promised, what save their greed prevented them from recognizing true blessings, and made them assume that blessings meant the riches of this world?

In truth, would even the cleverest people of the earth have understood this differently? They were slaves of the Romans; they were waiting for a redeemer who would make them victorious and who would make Jerusalem respected throughout the world. How, even with all their reason and insight, could they have recognized in Jesus, poor and hung on the cross, this conqueror and king? How could those to whom the Decalogue[6] had not mentioned the immortality of the soul have imagined a heavenly Jerusalem when they heard the name of their capital? Without some greater insight, how could a people so attached to its law have recognized in the prophecies, which were not part of their law, a god hidden in the form of a circumcised Jew, who by his new religion destroyed and made abominable both circumcision and the Sabbath, sacred foundations of Jewish law? Once again, let us adore God without trying to penetrate the obscurity of His mysteries.

XIII. The time of the first coming of Jesus Christ is predicted. The time of the second is not, for the first had to be hidden whereas the second will be dazzling and so manifest that even its enemies will recognize it.

The time of the second coming of Jesus Christ was predicted even more clearly than that of the first coming. M. Pascal had apparently forgotten that Jesus Christ, in the twenty-first chapter of Luke, said explicitly, "When you see Jerusalem surrounded by an army, know that the desolation is near . . . Jerusalem will be trodden underfoot, and there will be signs in the sun and the moon and the stars; the waves of the sea will make a great noise . . . The powers of the heavens shall be shaken; and then they will see the son of man, who will come in a cloud with great power and majesty."

Is this not the explicit prediction of the second coming? But, if this has not yet happened, it is not for us to dare interrogate Providence.

XIV. The Messiah, according to carnal Jews, is to be a great earthly prince. According to carnal Christians, he came to dispense us from *loving God*, and to give us sacraments that will *accomplish everything* without our effort. Neither of these is the true Christian or Jewish religion.

This section is more a satiric gibe than a Christian reflection. We see here that he is attacking the Jesuits. But in truth, did any Jesuit ever say that Jesus Christ *has come to dispense us from loving God?* The dispute about loving God is only a dispute about words, like most other scientific quarrels that have cause such lively hatred and such appalling harm.

There is yet another defect in this section. It assumes that awaiting the Messiah was a matter of Jewish doctrine. It was simply a consoling idea current throughout this nation. The Jews hoped for a redeemer. But they were not commanded to believe this as an article of faith. All their religion was set forth in the books of the Law. The Jews never considered the prophets as legislators.

XV. To examine the prophecies, one must understand them. For if one believes that they have only one meaning, it is certain that the Messiah has not come; but if they have two meanings, it is certain that he has come in the person of Jesus Christ.

The Christian religion is so true that it does not need dubious proofs; now, if something could shake the foundations of this holy and reasonable religion, it is this statement by M. Pascal. He insists that everything in Scripture has two meanings; but someone who had the misfortune to be an unbeliever could say to him: "He who gives two meanings to what he says intends to deceive men; and this duplicity is always punished by the law. How then could you without blushing accept in God those things that one punishes and detests in man? What am I saying? With what scorn and indignation do you not treat the oracles of pagans because they had two meanings! Might one not rather say that the prophecies that directly concern Jesus Christ have but one meaning, like those of Daniel, Micah, and others? Might one not even say that, even had we no knowledge of the prophecies, religion would be no less assured?"

XVI. The infinite distance between body and soul is a figure of the infinitely more infinite distance between souls and holy love, which is supernatural.

One might suspect that M. Pascal would not have used this nonsense in his work if he had had the time to write it.

XVII. The most obvious weaknesses are strengths for those who well understand things. For example, the two genealogies of Saint Matthew and Saint Luke: it is obvious that they were not made by collusion.

Should the editors of Pascal's *Pensées* have printed this thought, of which the exposition alone is perhaps capable of injuring religion? What is the use of saying that these genealogies, these fundamental elements of the Christian religion, contradict each other, without describing the ways in which they can be reconciled? One must give an antidote together with the poison. What would one think of an attorney who said: My client contradicts himself, but this weakness is a strength for those who can well understand such things?

XVIII. Then let no one continue to reproach us for this lack of clarity, since we freely admit it; but let them recognize the truth of religion, even in its obscurity, by what little light we do have, and in our lack of concern for understanding it.

What strange signs of truth does Pascal bring us! What other signs would falsehood propose? What! Would it be enough, if one wanted to be believed, to say: *I am obscure, I am incomprehensible!* It would be wiser to present only the illumination of faith, instead of the shadows of erudition.

XIX. If there were but one religion, God would be all too apparent.

What! You say that if there were but one religion God would be all too apparent! Eh! Do you forget that you say, on each page, that one day there will be but one religion? According to you, God will thus be all too apparent.

XX. I say that the Jewish religion consisted in none of these things, save only in the love of God and that God disapproved of all the other things.

What! Did God disapprove of everything that he himself so carefully, and in so much detail, commanded the Jews to do? Is it not more accurate to say that the law of Moses consisted both of love and of ritual? Reducing all to love of God would perhaps smack less of a love of God and more of the hatred that all Jansenists bear toward their neighbors the Molinists.[7]

> XXI. The most important thing in life is the choice of a profession; chance governs the matter; custom makes one a mason, soldier, roofer.

What else makes soldier, masons, and all manual laborers, if not what we call chance and custom? The only work one chooses for oneself is the work of the intellect, but it is quite natural and reasonable that custom should determine the work that most people do.

> XXII. If each one examines his thoughts, he will find himself always preoccupied by the past and the future. We scarcely think of the present; and if we do think about it, it is only to gain some insight so that we can plan the future. The present is never our goal; the past and the present are our means and only the future is our goal.

Rather than complaining, we must thank the creator of nature for having given us the instinct that unceasingly points us toward the future. Man's most precious treasure is this *hope* that softens our woes and paints our future pleasures in the colors of our present pleasures. If men were so unfortunate as to think only of the present, no one would sow grain, nor build, nor plant, nor provide for anything:[8] all would lack for everything in the midst of this illusory enjoyment. Could a mind like M. Pascal's give itself to a more foolish adage than this one? Nature has established that each man should enjoy the present, eating, making children, listening to beautiful sounds, using his abilities to think and to feel; and that, putting these aside even while he is in the midst of them, he should also think of tomorrow, without which he would perish miserably today.

> XXIII. But when I looked more closely, I found that man's reluctance to rest, and to reside within himself, comes from a most effective cause, that is to say from the natural misery of our feeble and mortal condition, a condition so miserable that nothing can console us if nothing prevents us from thinking of it and when we consider only ourselves.

This phrase *consider only ourselves* means nothing.

What could a man be who does not act, and who is presumed to contemplate himself? Not only do I say that such a man is an imbecile, useless to society, but also that such a man could not exist; for what would such a man contemplate, his body, his feet, his hands, his five senses? Either he would be an idiot or else he would be using all these things. Would he simply contemplate his ability to think? But he cannot contemplate this ability without using it. Either he will think of nothing, or he will think of ideas that he has already had, or he will invent new ones; now, he can only have ideas that come from outside him. Thus he is necessarily preoccupied either by his senses or by his ideas; thus he is either maddened or an idiot.

Once again, it is impossible for human nature to stay in this imagined stupefaction; it is ridiculous to think it could be; it is insane to aspire to it. Man is born for action as sparks fly upward and a stone drops. Not to be active and not to exist are the same thing for mankind.[9] The sole difference is in the activity, gentle or tumultuous, dangerous or useful.

XXIV. Man has a secret instinct that provokes him to look outside himself for diversion and work, that comes from his awareness of his continual misery; and he has another secret instinct, the vestiges of the greatness of his first condition, which makes him recognize that there is no happiness save in rest.

This secret instinct, being the first principle and the necessary foundation of society, comes rather from God's kindness. This instinct, and not the awareness of our misery, is the source of our happiness. I do not know what our first parents did in the earthly paradise, but if each of them had thought only of himself, the existence of the human race would have been much at risk. Is it not absurd to think that they had perfect senses, that is, perfect ability to act, and had them only for contemplative purposes? And is it not foolish for wise heads to imagine that laziness is an emblem of greatness, and that action cheapens our nature?

XXV. This is why, when Cinéas told Pyrrhus,[10] who intended to enjoy leisure with his friends once he had conquered a great part of the world, that he would do better to increase his well-being by enjoying his leisure now rather than by seeking it in so arduous a way, he gave advice full of difficulties, and that was scarcely more reasonable than the plans of the ambitious young man. Both believed that man, had he but himself and his possessions, could be content without filling the emptiness of his heart with imaginary hopes, which is false. Pyrrhus could not have been happy, either before or after having conquered the world.

The example of Cinéas is fine for the satires of [Boileau] but not for a philosophical book. A wise king can be happy at home; and since Pyrrhus is portrayed as a madman, the example proves nothing for the rest of humanity.

XXVI. We must recognize that man is so miserable that he would be bored even without any external cause, by the very nature of his condition.

On the contrary, man in this respect is fortunate, and we owe much to the author of nature who has made us bored with inaction, thus forcing us to be useful to our neighbors and ourselves.

XXVII. How does it happen that this man, who recently lost his only son and who, burdened with lawsuits and quarrels, was so distressed this morning, thinks no more of these things now? Do not be surprised: he is intent on seeing where a stag, which his dogs have been chasing for six hours, will emerge. That is all a man needs, however full of sorrow he may be. If one can persuade him to engage in some diversion, he will be happy as long as he does so.

This man does very well: dissipation is a better cure for sorrow than quinine is for fever; then let us not accuse nature, which is always ready to rescue us.

XXVIII. Imagine a number of men in chains, all condemned to death, some of whom are slaughtered each day in full view of the others; those who remain see their own condition in the fate of their fellows, and, looking at one another with anguish and without hope, await their turn. This is the image of the human condition.

This is assuredly an improper comparison; miserable men in chains, slaughtered one after another, are miserable not only because they suffer, but also because they experience what the other men do not. Man's natural fate is neither to be in chains nor to be slaughtered; but all men are made like animals and plants, to grow, to live for a certain time, to reproduce themselves, and to die. In a satire one may present man in a bad light as much as one wants; yet if one will but use his reason, he will admit that of all the animals man is the most perfect, the most fortunate, and the one that lives longest. Then instead of wondering at and complaining about misfortune and the shortness of life, we should wonder at and rejoice in our happiness and its duration. Simply reasoning as a philosopher, I dare to say that there is much pride and arrogance in suggesting that because of our nature we ought to be better than we are.

XXIX. Wise pagans who said there is but one God were persecuted; the Jew hated, and the Christians even more so.

At times they were persecuted, as would be today a man who came to preach the worship of one god, independent of accepted ritual. Socrates was not condemned for saying, *there is but one God*, but for having opposed the formal religion of his country, and for having ineptly made powerful enemies. As for the Jews, they were hated not because they believed in only one god, but because they foolishly hated the other nations; because they were barbarians who massacred their conquered enemies without pity; because this vile people, superstitious, ignorant, deprived of arts and commerce, scorned the more civilized nations.

As for the Christians, the pagans hated them because they tried to destroy both religion and the Empire, in which at last they succeeded; just as the Protestants became masters in those countries where they had long been hated, persecuted, and massacred.

XXX. Montaigne's defects are great. He uses filthy and improper words. That is worthless. His opinions on suicide and on death are horrible.[11]

Montaigne writes as a philosopher, not as a Christian; he is simply stating the *pro* and the *con* of suicide. Philosophically speaking, how does a man who can no longer serve society do harm by leaving it? An old man has the [kidney stones] and suffers unbearable pains because of it; someone says to him, "If you are not cut you will die; if you agree to be cut you might continue to mumble, drool, and drag through life for another year, a burden to yourself and to others." I imagine that the fellow would then choose to be no longer a burden to others; this is more or less the case that Montaigne describes.

XXXI. How many stars have the telescopes revealed to us that did not exist for earlier philosophers? People boldly attacked the Bible because it speaks in so many places of the great number of stars. There are but one thousand and twenty-two, said they; we know that.

It is certain that in discussing the physical world Holy Writ has always expressed itself in the language of its time; thus it asserts that the earth stands still, that the sun moves, etc. It did not state that the stars are innumerable because of refined astronomy, but because this was the common opinion. In fact, although our eyes can detect only a thousand and twenty-two stars, when we stare at the heavens our dazzled eyes seem to see an infinity of them. The Bible, then, expresses popular assumptions, for it was not given to us in order to make astronomers of us; and it is quite likely that God did not reveal to Habakkuk, to Baruch, or to Micah that one day an Englishman named Flamsteed[12] would put into his catalogue more than seven thousand stars observed by the telescope.

XXXII. Is it courageous for a dying man, in his weakness and agony, to defy an all-powerful and eternal God?

Such a thing has never happened, and only if he were out of his head could he say, "I believe in a god, and I defy him."

XXXIII. I gladly believe the stories whose witnesses let themselves be slaughtered.

The difficulty is not simply to know whether one will believe witnesses who died to uphold their beliefs, as many fanatics have done, but also to know whether indeed these witnesses died for this reason, whether their testimony has been preserved, whether they lived in the countries where they are said to have died. Why is it that Josephus, born in the time of Christ's death, Josephus the enemy of Herod, Josephus so indifferent to Judaism, did not say one word about it? This is what M. Pascal ought to have successfully explained, as have so many eloquent writers since his day.

XXXIV. The two extremes of the sciences meet. One of them is pure natural ignorance, in which all men find themselves at birth; the other extreme is the one reached by those great souls who, having examined all that man can know, discover that they know nothing and find themselves again in the ignorance from whence they departed.

This reflection is mere sophistry, and its falseness lies in the word *ignorance*, which one can understand in two ways. He who knows not how to read and write is ignorant; but a mathematician, who may not know the hidden principles of nature, is not at the point of ignorance from which he departed when he began to learn to read. M. Newton did not know how man can move his arm when he wishes to, but he was not less learned about all other things. He who knows not Hebrew but who knows Latin is learned by comparison with him who knows only French.

XXXV. Being happy does not consist in being delighted by diversions, for they come from somewhere else and outside; thus happiness is dependent and subject to being disturbed by the thousand accidents that make afflictions inevitable.

He who has pleasure is happy at that moment, and this pleasure can only come from without. Only external objects can give us sensations and ideas, just as we can only nourish our bodies by ingesting foreign substances that are changed into our own.

XXXVI. Great genius, and its absence, are condemned as folly. Only mediocrity is considered good.

Not great genius but excess of vivacity and volubility is condemned as folly. Great genius means great judgment, great precision, great breadth of knowledge, all of which are diametrically different from madness.

Great *absence of intellect* means a defect of imagination, a lack of ideas; this is not madness but stupidity. Madness is a disorder of the organs that prompts one to see too many things too quickly, or that excessively and violently concentrates the imagination on a single object. Nor is it mediocrity that is considered good, but rather the rejection of the two extremes; this is the *golden mean*, not *mediocrity*.

XXXVII. If our condition were truly happy, we would not need to distract ourselves from thinking about it.

Our condition is precisely to think about external things, with which we have a necessary relationship. It is false to think that one can distract a person from thinking about the human condition, for no matter what he thinks about, he thinks of something necessarily linked to the human condition; and, once again, beware: to think of oneself apart from natural things means thinking about nothing, truly about nothing.

Far from hindering a man from thinking about his condition, we talk to him of nothing but his good qualities. We speak to a learned man about his reputation and his knowledge, to a prince about what befits his grandeur, and to everyone we speak of pleasure.

XXXVIII. Great men and lesser ones are subject to the same accidents, annoyances, and passions. But the former are at the top of the wheel, the others closer to the center and thus less upset by the same dislocations.

It is false that lesser men are less upset than great ones; on the contrary, their despair is greater because they have fewer resources. Of one hundred men who kill themselves in London, ninety-nine are of low condition, and scarcely one of the upper class. The image of the wheel is ingenious and misleading.

XXXIX. Men are not taught to be honorable, although they are taught everything else, and yet they take pride only in that. Thus, they take pride in knowing the only thing that they have not learned.

Men are taught to be honorable, and without that, few would become such. Let your son as a child take whatever comes to hand, and at fifteen he will be a highwayman. Praise him for telling a lie, and he will bear false witness; encourage his desires, and he will surely be debauched. Men are taught everything—virtue, religion.

XL. What a stupid project Montaigne undertook to paint himself! Not as an aside, forgetting his tenets, as all men do, but intentionally revealing himself in the light of his own principles; for, saying stupid things by chance or carelessly is a common mistake, but deliberately to report such stupid things is intolerable.

What a charming project is Montaigne's—to depict himself naively as he has done! For he depicts human nature itself; and how feeble of Nicole,[13] of Malebranche, of Pascal, to attempt to disparage Montaigne.

XLI. When I reflect on the reason that we put so much trust in so many imposters who say that they have remedies, even to the point of putting our lives in their hands, it seems to me that the reason for this is that true remedies do exist; for it does not seem possible that there would be so many false remedies, and that they could be believed, if there were no true ones. If there had never been such true remedies, if all evils had been incurable, men could not possibly believe that they could concoct cures, and it is even more impossible that others would have trusted those who boasted of having them. Similarly, if a man boasted of being able to prevent death, no one would believe him, because there is no instance of such a thing. But numbers of real cures have been found and recognized even by the wisest of men, and this fact has shaped our belief. The existence of remedies cannot be generally denied since some have been shown to be effective; thus the people, who cannot distinguish which of them are true, believe them all. Likewise, people believe false theories of the moon's influences because some of them, such as the tides, are true.

And it seems to me equally evident that there are so many false claims of miracles, revelations, enchantments, because some are real.

It seems to me that human nature does not need the truth in order to fall into falsehood. Men mistakenly claimed a thousand influences of the moon before imagining even the least relationship between the moon and the tides. The first man who was ill easily believed the first charlatan. No one has seen a werewolf or a sorcerer, and many have believed in them. No one has witnessed the transmutation of metals, and many have been ruined by their belief in the philosopher's stone. Did the Romans, the Greeks, all the pagans believe in the false miracles with which they were inundated only because they had witnessed some that were true?

XLII. The harbormaster governs those who are aboard a ship, but where do we find an equivalent for our moral code?

In this one maxim, acknowledged by all nations:
"Do not do to the other what you would not have done to yourself."

XLIII. *Ferox gens nullam esse vitam sine armis putat.*[14] They prefer death to peace; the others prefer death to war. Any opinion can be preferred to life, the love of which is so strong and so natural.

Tacitus said this of the Catalans, but there have never been any of whom one has said or could say, "They prefer death to war."

XLIV. The more intelligence one has, the more one recognizes originality in men. Ordinary people see no differences among them.

There are very few truly original men; almost all govern themselves, think, and feel as a result of custom and education. Nothing is so unusual as a mind that walks a new path; but in this crowd of men who march together, each has a slightly different way of proceeding, which a sharp eye will recognize.

XLV. There are thus two kinds of minds: one that sees the consequences of first principles clearly and deeply, and that is the just mind, and one that understands many different principles without confusing them, and this is the geometer's mind.

Nowadays, I believe, we might call *the geometer's mind* the methodical and reasoning mind.

XLVI. It is easier to bear death when one does not think about it than it is to think about death when one is not in peril.

One cannot say that a man bears death easily or with difficulty when he is not thinking about it. Who feels nothing bears nothing.

XLVII. We believe that all men conceive of and are aware of objects in the same way; but we believe this quite arbitrarily, even though we have no proof of it. I clearly see that people use the same words in the same circumstances, and that each time two men see snow, for instance, they both express the sight of the object using the same words, saying that snow is white; and from this conformity of expression we derive a strong assumption of a conformity of ideas; but this is not perfectly convincing even if there is reason to wager that it is true.

One should not use whiteness as proof. White, which is a mixture of all rays of light, shines brilliantly, eventually dazzles, and has the same effect on all eyes; but one might say that perhaps other colors are not seen the same way by all eyes.

XLVIII. All our reasoning in the end yields to feelings.

Our reasoning gives way to feelings in matters of taste, not in matters of science.

XLIX. Those who judge a work by rules are, with respect to others, like those who have a watch compared to those who do not have one. One says, "We have been here for two hours," another says, "It has only been three quarters of an hour." I look at my watch: I say to the first, "You are bored," and to the second, "Time goes quickly for you."

In matters of taste, music, poetry, painting, taste takes the place of the watch, and someone who judges only by rules judges badly.

> L. Caesar was too old, in my opinion, to go off and entertain himself by conquering the world. This entertainment was good for Alexander; he was a young man whom it was difficult to stop; but Caesar should have been more mature.

Ordinarily we assume that Alexander and Caesar left home with the intention of conquering the world, but it was not that way at all: Alexander succeeded Philip as the commander of Greece, and had been charged with the legitimate task of taking vengeance for the injuries inflicted by the king of Persia upon the Greeks; he fought their common enemy and continued his conquests as far as India because the kingdom of Darius extended to India; just as the Duke of Marlborough would have come as far as Lyon had it not been for Marshal de Villars.[15]

As for Caesar, he was one of the most prominent men of the Republic. He quarreled with Pompey as the Jansenists quarreled with the Molinists; the question was who would exterminate the other. One single battle, in which barely ten thousand men were killed, decided everything.

Indeed, M. Pascal's reflections may be altogether false. Caesar's maturity was necessary to cope with so many intrigues; and it is astonishing that Alexander, at his age, should have renounced pleasure to undertake so difficult a war.

> LI. It is amusing to think that there are men in this world—for example, robbers and so on—who, having rejected all the laws of God and nature, have made their own laws that they obey most meticulously.

It is even more useful than amusing to think this, for it proves that no human society can survive without laws for a single day.

> LII. Man is neither an angel nor a beast; the misery is that whoever wishes to play the angel becomes a beast.

Whoever wants to destroy the passions, rather than governing them, wants to play the *angel*.

> LIII. A horse does not seek to have its companion admire him; when they race we see some kind of emulation in them, but it is not significant; for, once in the stable, the heaviest and the least shapely does

not give up his hay to the others. Men are not like this: their ability does not satisfy them, and they are not content unless they gain some advantage from it over the others.

The most ungainly man does not surrender his bread to others; but the stronger takes it from the weaker; and it is with animals as it is with men: the large eat the small.

LIV. If man were to begin by studying himself he would see how incapable he is of going beyond himself. How can a part know the whole? He might hope perhaps to know the parts to which he has some resemblance. But all the parts of the world have so much connection and involvement with one another that I believe it impossible to know one thing unless one knows the others, and the whole.

Man must not be discouraged from seeking what is useful for him, simply because he cannot know everything.

> Even if you cannot see as clearly as Lynceus
> You should not hesitate to wash your bleary eyes.[16]

We know many things that are true; we have sought out many useful inventions. Let us comfort ourselves even if we do not know the connections between a spider and the rings of Saturn, and continue to examine what is in our grasp.

LV. If lightning fell on low places, poets and those who know how to think only about such matters would be at a loss for proofs.

A comparison is not a proof either in poetry or in prose: in poetry it is a kind of embellishment, and in prose it serves to clarify and to make matters more vivid. Poets who have compared the misfortunes of the great with the lightning that strikes mountains would construct different comparisons if different things happened.

LVI. It is this mixture of spirit and body that has caused almost all philosophers to confuse ideas, and to attribute to the body what pertains only to the spirit, and to spirit what can only apply to the body.

If we knew what *spirit* is, we could complain about the fact that philosophers have attributed to it what does not belong to it, but we know neither spirit nor body. We have no knowledge of one, and we have only imperfect knowledge of the other, thus we cannot know what are their limits.

LVII. As people say *poetic beauty*, they should also speak of *geometric beauty* and *medicinal beauty*. But we do not say this; and the reason is that we know the objects of geometry or medicine very well, but we do not know what makes up the harmony that is the object of poetry. We do not understand the natural model that we must imitate; and lacking such knowledge we have invented bizarre terms: *golden age, the wonder of the age, deadly laurel, magnificent star*, etc., and we call this jargon poetic beauty. But someone imagining a woman clothed in these terms would see a pretty girl all covered with mirrors and chains of brass.

This is quite false: one should not say *geometric beauty* or *medicinal beauty*, because a theorem and a purgative do not give a pleasant impression, and one uses the word *beauty* only for things that charm the senses, like music, painting, eloquence, poetry, symmetrical architecture, etc.

M. Pascal's reason is equally false. We know very well what is the object of poetry: it is to paint with strength, precision, delicacy, and harmony; poetry is harmonious eloquence. M. Pascal must have had very little taste to say that *deadly laurel, magnificent star*, and other foolishness is poetic beauty; and it must be that the editors of these *Pensées* were people little versed in literature if they printed a comment so unworthy of its illustrious author.

I do not send you my other comments on M. Pascal's *Pensées*, which would require much too much discussion. It is enough to have tried to point out a few of this great genius's mistakes of inattention; it is a consolation for a mind as limited as mine to be persuaded that the greatest of men make mistakes like the rest of us.

PROPOSAL FOR A LETTER ABOUT THE ENGLISH

[Projet d'une lettre sur les Anglais]

Probable date: 1728

Yesterday I came by chance upon a bad book by a certain Dennis—for there are also bad writers among the English. This author, in a little report of a fifteen days' stay in France, pretends to depict the character of the nation that he had so much time to observe. "I will," said he, "give you a true and natural portrait of the French, and I will commence by telling you that I mortally hate them. In truth, they received me very well, and overwhelmed me with civility; but all that is pure arrogance, it is not to please us that they receive us so kindly, it is to please themselves; it is a very ridiculous nation! Etc."[1]

Pray don't imagine that all the English think as this Mr. Dennis does, nor that I have the least desire to imitate him when I speak to you about the English nation, as you have bidden me to do.

You would like to have me give you a general idea of the people among whom I live. These general ideas are subject to too many exceptions: moreover, a traveler but imperfectly knows the country in which he finds himself. He sees only the façade of the building; almost all its interior is unknown. You might think that an ambassador is always well informed about the genius of the people to whom he has been sent, and would be able to tell you more about it than other men. That may be true of foreign ministers who live in Paris, for they all know the language of the country; they are engaged with a nation that easily reveals itself; they are received, to the extent that they wish it, by all levels of society, all of which are eager to please him; they read our books; they go to our theaters. A French ambassador in England is quite different. Ordinarily he knows not a word of English; without an interpreter he cannot converse with three quarters of the nation; he has not the least idea of the works written in its language; he cannot see the plays that reveal its customs. The very small number of clubs to which he might be admitted are of a character that differs markedly from the openness of the French; people gather in them to play cards or to be silent. Because the

123

nation is for the most part divided into two parties, the ambassador could not be connected with members of the opposition for fear of being suspect; he is reduced to meeting only the ministers of state, and is a bit like a merchant who knows only those with whom he does business, with this difference: that a merchant, to succeed, must act honestly, behavior that does not always figure among His Excellency's instructions. The result is that often an ambassador is a kind of canal through which lies and political deceptions flow from one court to the other, and who, having for some years ceremoniously told lies in the name of the king his master, departs forever from a nation that he does not know at all.

It may be that you will be able to gain more light from a private person who has enough leisure and stubbornness to learn to speak English, who speaks freely with Whigs and Tories, who dines with a bishop and sups with a Quaker, who goes on Saturday to the synagogue and on Sunday to Saint Paul's, who listens to a sermon in the morning and goes to a comedy in the afternoon, who moves from the Court to the Exchange, who will not be dismayed by the cool, disdainful, and icy demeanor with which ladies begin an acquaintance, and which at times they never abandon; a man such as the one I describe would yet be capable of being mistaken, of giving you incorrect ideas, especially if he were to judge, as one ordinarily does, on the basis of a first glance.

When I landed in London, it was in the middle of spring; the sky was cloudless, as it is on the loveliest days in the south of France; the air was made fresh by a gentle west wind, which enhanced the serenity of nature, and prepared us for delight: so much are we *machines*, and so much do our souls depend on the movements of our bodies. I stopped near Greenwich, on the banks of the Thames. On this beautiful river, which never floods and whose banks are ornamented with plants all year long, floated two lines of merchant vessels for a distance of six miles; all had spread their sails to honor the King and Queen who, seated on a golden barge, were taking a turn on the river, preceded by boats full of musicians and followed by a thousand little rowboats; each manned by two oarsmen clad, like our pages in earlier times, in breeches and in little jerkins ornamented with a large silver brooch on the shoulder. Their faces, their clothes and their robustness all advertised that they were free men who lived in a world of plenty.

Near the river, on a grand lawn that extends for about four miles, I saw an enormous number of handsome young men cantering around a sort of racecourse marked by white stakes planted in the ground mile after mile. There were also young women on horseback galloping here and there most gracefully; and, in particular, young girls on foot, clothed for the most part in India cloth. Many were very beautiful, all were good looking, they had about them an air of neatness, vivacity and contentment that made them all appear pretty.

Another little racecourse was set in the larger one: it was about five hundred feet long, and ended in a little balustrade. I asked what that was for. I learned soon that the large course was devoted to horse races, and the smaller one to foot races. Near one of the posts of the large course was a man on horseback, who held a kind of large covered silver pitcher; at the balustrade at the end of the smaller course were two poles: on the top of one a large hat was hanging, and on the other, a lady's pelisse. A tall man stood between the two poles, holding a purse in his hand. The large silver pitcher was the prize for the horse race; the purse was the prize for the foot race; but I was pleasantly surprised when I was told that there was also a race for the young girls; that the winner, to mark her victory, was given a purse and the pelisse that waved at the top of the pole, and that the hat was for the man who had run the fastest.

I had the good fortune to discover in the crowd some merchants to whom I had letters of introduction. These gentlemen welcomed me to the festivities with the eagerness and cordiality of those who are happy and who wish others to be so as well. They brought me a horse, they sent for refreshments, they took care to place me where I could easily see all the races, the river, and a view of London in the distance.

I felt I had been transported to the Olympic games, but the beauty of the Thames, this flotilla of ships, the immensity of the city of London, made me blush when I thought of my comparison of ancient Elis with England.[2] I learned that there was at the same time a boxing match,[3] and straightaway I thought myself in ancient Rome. A messenger from Denmark, who had arrived that morning and who was fortunately to return that very evening, found himself near me during the races. He seemed to be overcome by joy and astonishment; he believed that all the nation were always gay, that all the women were beautiful and lively, and that the English sky was always clear and serene; that people thought only of pleasure; that every day was like the one he had seen; and he left undeceived. As for me, even more delighted than my Dane, I was presented that evening to several ladies of the Court; I spoke only of the beautiful spectacle from which I had come; I did not doubt that they had been there, and that they had been among those whom I saw riding with such grace.

However, I was a trifle surprised to see that they did not have the air of vivacity common to those who have been enjoying themselves; they were stiff and cold, drank tea, rattled their fans, spoke not a word or chattered malicious gossip to each other in shrill voices; some played quadrille,[4] others read the latest gazette; at last one of the more charitable among them was kind enough to tell me that the best society did not stoop to attend those common gatherings that had charmed me so much; that all those lovely women dressed in India cloth were servants or country folk; that all those brilliant young people, mounted on such fine horses and riding with such skill around the racecourse, were students and apprentices on horses they had hired. I felt truly angry with the lady who told me all that. I tried to believe none of it; and returned in vexation to the City, in search of the merchants and the aldermen who had so cordially welcomed me to my so-called Olympic games.

The next morning, in a dirty coffee house, ill-furnished, ill-attended, and poorly lit, I found most of those gentlemen who the evening before were so affable and so good-humored; none of them recognized me; I dared to address a few words to some of them; I got from them no response, or at best a "yes" or a "no"; I assumed that I had offended them all the day before. I examined my conscience and tried to remember whether I had boasted about cloth from Lyons and disparaged theirs; or whether I had said that French cooks were better than English ones; that Paris was a more pleasant city than London; that one spent time more agreeably at Versailles than at the Court of St. James; or made some other equally outrageous remark. Not finding myself guilty, I took the liberty of asking one of them, with a vivacity that seemed very strange to them, why they all seemed so somber; my man replied in a chilly voice that it was because the wind was in the east. At that moment one of their friends arrived, who said with a calm expression, "Molly cut her throat this morning. Her lover found her dead in her room, with a bloody razor next to her." This Molly was a pretty young woman, very rich, who was about to marry the very man who had found her dead. These gentlemen, who were all friends of Molly, received the news without blinking. One of them simply asked what had become of the lover; *he bought the razor*, said one of those present.

I, terrified by so strange a death and by the indifference of these gentlemen, could not refrain from asking the reasons why a young woman, apparently so fortunate, should have so cruelly ended her life; the only answer I received was that the wind was in the east. I could not at first understand what the east wind had to do with the

somber mood of these gentlemen and the death of Molly. I left the
coffee house abruptly and went to the Court, full of that fine French
assumption that there one is always gay. There all was gloomy, even
to the ladies in waiting who spoke in melancholy tones about the east
wind. I thought then about the Danish fellow of the past evening. I
was tempted to laugh about the mistaken impression of England that
he had taken away with him; but the climate was having its effect on
me, and I was surprised to find that I could not laugh. A famous
court physician to whom I confided my surprise told me I was wrong
to be astonished; that I should see a quite different world in
November and in March; that people at those times hanged themselves by the dozens; that almost everyone was truly ill in those sea-
sons; and that black melancholy spread over the land; for 'tis then,
said he, that the east wind blows constantly. This wind is the undo-
ing of our island. Even the animals suffer in it, and all of them look
beaten down. Indeed, even those men who are robust enough to stay
healthy during this damn'd wind lose their good humor when it
blows.[5] Each one looks severe, and his spirit disposes him to desper-
ate resolves. It was in fact during an east wind that Charles I was
beheaded, and James II deposed. "If you wish to ask a favor at court,"
he whispered in my ear, "do not do so unless the wind is in the west
or south."

In addition to the difficulties imposed on the English by the elements are those that are born from the animosities of political parties; it is this that most disorients a foreigner.

I have explicitly heard it said that Milord Marlborough was the
greatest coward in the world;[6] and that Pope was a dunce.[7]

I had arrived believing that a Whig was a proud republican, enemy
of the crown; and a Tory a believer in passive obedience. But I found
that in the Parliament almost all the Whigs were for the Court, and
the Tories against it.

One day, traveling on the Thames, one of my oarsmen, seeing that
I was French, began to boast proudly of the freedom in his country,
swearing to God that he would prefer to be a boatman on the
Thames than an archbishop in France. The next day I saw this same
fellow in a prison I was passing by; he had shackles on his feet and
was stretching out his hand through the bars to passers-by. I asked
him whether he still thought so little of a French archbishop; he recognized me. "Ah, Sir, what an abominable government is this! I was
impressed to serve in Norway on the king's ship; they snatched me
from my wife and my children, and threw me into prison with shackles on my feet for fear that I should flee before the day of sailing."[8]

The sorrow of this man, and this brazen injustice, touched me deeply. A Frenchman who was with me admitted that he felt a malignant delight upon seeing that the English, who so haughtily condemn our lack of freedom, were just as much slaves as we. I had a more humane reaction: I was deeply distressed to see that nowhere on earth is there freedom.

Full of bitterness, I had written a letter to you on this topic when an act of Parliament ended the abuse of impressing seamen by force, and made me throw my letter into the fire.[9] To give you a stronger idea of the contradictions I have been discussing, I tell you that I saw four very learned treatises denying the miracles of Jesus Christ, at the same time that a small bookshop was condemned for having published a translation of *The Nun in her Smock*.[10]

They promised me that I would find my Olympic games at Newmarket. "All the nobility," I learned, "come there twice a year. Even the King and the royal family come from time to time. There you will see little jockeys clad in silk riding a prodigious number of the swiftest horses in Europe, all bred of Arab stallions and English mares, which, under the eyes of the whole Court, fly along a racetrack of green grass that extends as far as the eye can see." I went to find this elegant spectacle, and I saw horse traders of high rank disparaging one another, and adding knavery rather than magnificence to this solemn occasion.[11]

Shall I move from trifles to larger matters? I will ask you whether it is easy to describe a nation that beheaded Charles I because he wanted to introduce the surplice into Scotland, and because he levied a tax to which the judges declared he was entitled; while this same nation watched, without a murmur, while Cromwell dissolved the Parliament, removed the lords and the bishops, and overturned all the laws.

Reflect on the fact that James II was deposed in part because he insisted on appointing a Catholic pedant to the university;[12] and remember that Henry VIII, that bloody tyrant, half Catholic, half Protestant, changed the religion of the country because he wished to marry a shameless woman whom he later sent to the scaffold;[13] that he wrote a bad book against Luther and in support of the Pope, then made himself pope in England, hanging all those who denied his supremacy and burning those who did not believe in transubstantiation; and doing all this with glee and impunity.[14]

A spirit of religious enthusiasm, of frantic superstition, seized the nation during the civil wars; and this time of trouble was followed, during the reign of Charles II, by weak and lazy impiety.

So all things change, and events contradict each other. What is truth at one time is error in another. The Spanish say of a man, *he was brave yesterday*. This is more or less the way one should speak of nations, and especially of the English: one should say, "They were thus in such a year, in that month."

Notes

Introduction

1 The Duchy reverted to the French crown upon the death, in 1766, of the last duke, Stanislaus Leszcynski, formerly king of Poland and the son-in-law of Louis XV.

2 For example, Charles de Brosses, who traveled to Venice in the next decade, reports that traveling on the Grand Canal was just like entering Paris or Lyons on the river (Charles de Brosses, Letter of 14 August 1739, *Lettres d' Italie, 1739–1740.*)

3 The first full edition of Voltaire's history of the seventeenth century, *Le siècle de Louis XIV*, was published in 1751.

4 Denis Diderot (1713–1784) and Jean le Rond d'Alembert (1717–1783) were the chief editors of the *Encyclopédie*, first published in 1751. It is considered an important manifestation of Enlightenment accomplishments and ambitions.

5 Voltaire provided hospitality to countless visitors, many of whom were English, and at Ferney in France, near Geneva where he settled in 1759, he earned the nickname "the innkeeper of Europe."

6 For a considered view of Pascal, his *Pensées*, and his reception in the eighteenth century, see *The Cambridge Companion to Pascal*, ed. Nicholas Hammond (Cambridge: Cambridge University Press, 2003).

7 See David Wootton, "Unhappy Voltaire, or 'I Shall Never Get Over It as Long as I Live,'" *History Workshop Journal*, vol. 50 (2000), 137–55.

8 Roland Barthes, "The Last Happy Writer" in *Critical Essays*, trans. Richard Howard (Evanston, Ill., 1972), 83–89.

Translator's Note

1 *Letters Concerning the English Nation by Mr. De Voltaire* [London: 1733]; *Lettres philosophiques par M. de V.*

2 *A View of Sir Isaac Newton's Philosophy.* Isaac Pemberton [London, printed by S. Palmer: 1728].

3 Voltaire: *Lettres philosophiques*, Édition présentée, établie et annoté par Fréderic Deloffre [Paris, Gallimard: 1986].

First Letter

1 Critics have identified the Quaker as Andrew Pitt, possibly a draper, but Voltaire does not reveal his name—the better to make wider comments

about the Quakers. Pitt seems to have lived in Hampstead. See André-Michel Rousseau, *L'Angleterre et Voltaire (1718–1789)* (Oxford: Voltaire Foundation, 1976), 3 vols.

2 Voltaire draws attention to a further characteristic—that of not removing hats to anyone. This refusal caused William Penn (1644–1718) to be fined for contempt of court while on trial in 1670. See Mary Maples Dunn, "The Personality of William Penn," *Proceedings of the American Philosophical Society*, 127, no.5 (1983) 316–321.

3 Quakers retained the use of the second person singular "thou" and its corresponding forms, an otherwise anachronistic practice by the eighteenth century, except in poetry.

4 The Huguenots were expelled from France when Louis XIV revoked the Edict of Nantes in 1685. Voltaire's hero, Henri IV, had promulgated the Edict in 1598, granting Protestants the freedom to worship.

5 In fact, the Quaker quotes accurately Matthew 3:11 and 1 Corinthians 1:17.

6 Robert Barclay (1648–1690) published *Catechism and Confession of Faith* (1673) and *An Apology for the True Christian Divinity* (1676), probably the book which Voltaire promises to read. Imprisoned several times, Barclay was, in 1683, chosen to be governor for life of the province of East New Jersey in America.

7 Augustus restrained the use of fulsome titles, would not sanction the erection of altars to himself, and forbade his statue to be placed among those of the gods. However, his policies seem soon to have been reversed. M.P. Charlesworth, "Deus Noster Caesar" *The Classical Review*. Vol. 39 (1925), 113–115.

Second Letter

1 *The Monument* was erected in memory of the Great Fire of London, 1666, whose causes were understood variously to be gluttony and popery. The meeting house on Gracechurch Street, which runs north of the monument, was at the center of a large Quaker business community in the city of London. Voltaire calls the meeting house an "église or chapelle" in his French, no doubt despairing of finding an exact equivalent.

2 A philosopher and theologian, Nicolas Malebranche (1638–1715) argued that the real nature of the external world must be found in ideas. Since the mind cannot produce its own ideas, for their creation requires a greater force, we see all things in God.

Third Letter

1 George Fox (1624–1691) was founder of the Society of Friends. Voltaire probably derives this information from Fox's *Journal*, published in 1694.

2 Quakers shared the republican views of Oliver Cromwell (1599–1658), Lord Protector, but were still treated with suspicion.

3 The Italian here is highly ambiguous. Some scholars argue that "fornication" is a twentieth century appropriation and that the passage should be translated as "Where no one was locked in," referring to the "locking in" of cardinals as they decided who would become the next Pope. However, Voltaire generally moves into Italian when he is speaking in sexual terms (see *Candide* and correspondence with his niece); as such, "Where there is no fornicating" more likely conveys Voltaire's intended meaning.

4 Charles II (1630–1685) who came to the throne in 1660, continued to persecute the Quakers.

5 Robert Barclay, *Apology for the True Christian Divinity* (1676).

Fourth Letter

1 William Penn, founder of Pennsylvania, wrote numerous works, which were collected in an edition of 1726 and published by Joseph Besse.

2 In the second edition of his book *No Cross, No Crown* (1669), Penn celebrated the piety of Elizabeth of Bohemia, Princess Palatine (1618–1680) who corresponded with René Descartes (1596–1650). Voltaire uses the phrase "roman de philosophie" to describe the *Principles of Philosophy* (*Principia Philosophical*) which he dedicated to her.

3 A characteristic Voltairean reflection on the accursed fortunes of the Stuarts. Voltaire saw a pattern in the destinies of Mary Queen of Scots (executed in 1587), James II (deposed in 1688) and Charles Edward Stuart (later, Bonnie Prince Charlie).

4 This may mean either British pounds or "pieces" of gold. No French currency in the eighteenth century was called a *pièce*; *pièce* simply meant "coin." Modern translators suggest that Voltaire is referring to the British pound sterling.

5 It is true that the British took direct control of Pennsylvania between 1692 and 1694, when Penn's loyalty to James II resulted in a charge of treason. But his proprietorship was restored in 1692, and he and his heirs retained it until the American Revolution.

Fifth Letter

1 Queen Anne reigned from 1702 to 1714.

2 Guelphs and Ghibellines were antagonistic factions in Germany and in Italy during the later Middle Ages. The names were used to denote the papal supporters (Guelphs) and the imperial party (Ghibellines) during the long struggle between popes and the Holy Roman emperors.

3 Robert Harley, first Earl of Oxford (1661–1724) and Henry St. John, Viscount Bolingbroke (1678–1751), influential figures in the reign of Queen Anne.

4 The House of Lords consists of Lords Temporal and Lords Spiritual. The latter are made up of the Archbishop of Canterbury and York, the bishops of London, Durham, and Winchester, and a selection of bishops drawn from other dioceses.

5 Pierre François le Courayer (1681–1776) was fêted in England after fleeing from France, where he was faced with a possible trial for heresy. He had published a *Dissertation sur la validité des ordinations des anglois* in 1723, which was translated in 1725. The work provoked hostility, above all from the Jesuits.

6 The consecration of Matthew Parker (1504–1525) as Archbishop of Canterbury was controversial. Although the fable that Parker was consecrated at a mock service held in the Nag's Head Tavern in London's Cheapside has long since been discredited, there were reservations concerning its legal status. The validity of orders within the Church of England continued to be questioned in the following centuries.

7 Another reference to Henry St. John, Viscount Bolingbroke, whom Voltaire met when the Englishman was exiled in France. In his *Letters on the Study and Use of History*, his attacks on church history provoked hostility. Whereas most Protestant writers denied the idea of apostolic succession (the notion that the ministry of the Christian church is derived from the apostles by a continuous succession and maintained by a series of bishops), the Anglican church shared the Roman Catholic conviction.

8 The role of the *abbé* is notoriously difficult to define. See the discussion in John McManners, *Church and Society in Eighteenth-Century France* (Oxford: Oxford University Press, 2000), 2 vols.; I, 647–82.

9 From chapter 22, 3rd *Book of Pantagruel* by François Rabelais (*c*.1490–1553).

Sixth Letter

1 Geneva, where Voltaire settled in 1755, was synonymous with the Reformation. "I do not decide between Geneva and Rome," says Henri IV in the second canto of Voltaire's *Henriade*.

2 Diogenes "the Cynic" (*c*.412–323 BCE) is supposed simply to have asked Alexander the Great to move out of the light when they met. Voltaire repeatedly labels his rival and proud Genevan Jean-Jacques Rousseau (1712–1778) a "Diogenes." See, for example, letters 10507, 10515, 10598, 11208 in Voltaire's *Correspondence, Complete Works of Voltaire*.

3 Cato Uticensis (95–46 BCE), a model of political rectitude and austerity, and the subject of a play by Joseph Addison (1672–1719) in 1713 that was a great success, particularly in America. See Ahmed Gunny, "Some Eighteenth-Century Reactions to Plays on the Life of Cato," *British Journal of Eighteenth-Century Studies* 4 (1981) 54–65.

4 The 1733 translation claims that "ministers are so fortunate as to enjoy a revenue of five or six thousand pounds," a figure much more plausible than Voltaire's fifty thousand.

5 An allusion to England, Scotland, and Wales, even though they were collectively governed by King and Parliament.

6 The Royal Exchange was set up in 1566 and became a foremost European trading center. It was rebuilt on the same site in the nineteenth century after being destroyed by fire.

Seventh Letter

1 In the fourth century, Athanasius introduced a creed that became the basis for Catholic doctrine. Arians and Socinians held heretical views about the Trinity and the divinity of Christ.

2 The source of this anecdote appears to be the Jesuit historian Louis Maimbourg (1610–1686) in Maimbourg, *History of Arianism*, translated by William Webster (London: Roberts, 1728–1729) 2 vols., I, 611–612.

3 Samuel Clarke (1675–1729) was renowned for his encyclopaedic knowledge and the wide range of his philosophical and theological interests. See W.H. Barber, "Voltaire and Samuel Clarke," *Studies on Voltaire and the Eighteenth Century*, 129 (1929), 47–61.

4 This remark can be attributed to Henry St. John, Viscount Bolingbroke.

5 In addition to Isaac Newton (1642–1727), John Locke (1632–1704) and Samuel Clarke whom Voltaire has just mentioned, he includes a passing reference to Jean Le Clerc (1657–1736), a theologian and philosopher who disseminated the ideas of figures such as Locke and Newton.

6 Jean Francois Paul de Conti, Cardinal de Retz (1614–1679), took a leading part in the troubled Crown during the *Fronde*.

7 In a similar vein, Thomas Gray (1716–1771) in his *Elegy Written in a Country Churchyard* imagined "some Cromwell, guiltless of his country's blood."

Eighth Letter

1 William Shippen (1673–1743), member of Parliament, who, in 1718, was sent to the Tower of London for speaking words that reflected badly on George I.

2 John Milton had spoken of "the majesty of the English people" exhibited when they toppled Charles I in his *Defence of the People of England* (London, 1651). The phrase originated in Tacitus' *Annals* Book 1, 70.

3 Criminal courts held periodically around England and Wales.

4 Voltaire is alluding to the battles in the War of the Spanish Succession which pitted Louis XIV (1643–1715) against British forces.

5 A prominent Catholic family that wielded particular influence in the reigns of Charles IX (1560–1574) and Henry III (1574–1589).

6 Jules Mazarin (1602–1661), advisor to Louis XIV, monarch during the *Fronde*.

7 Charles VI's reign (1380–1422) was vitiated by feuds between the Royal Family and the House of Burgundy. The League, allied to the Guises, opposed the Protestants in the sixteenth century. Voltaire observed that most wars fought by Christian monarchs were "sorts of civil wars." *Oeuvres historiques* (Paris: Gallimard, 1957), p.786.

8 Emperor Henry VII, who died in 1313, is said to have been poisoned by a priest while at Holy Communion. Henry III of France was assassinated in 1589 by Jacques Clément, a Dominican. Henry IV was assassinated in his turn by François Ravaillac, whom Voltaire saw as guilty of religious fanaticism. Voltaire was frequently haunted by such inventories of the victims of religious fanaticism.

Ninth Letter

1 The reign of William the Conqueror, (1066–1087) is likely to have been extremely authoritarian. But in the later *Essais sur les moeurs* (I, 470), Voltaire changes his mind about the rules instituted by William, which, "far from being tyrannical, were but an ancient policy in most northern towns" to protect against fire.

2 There seems to have been no Anglo-Saxon king of the Heptarchy named Inas. It is King Offa who, in 787, is said to have been the first to have paid "Peter's Pence" (the one-penny tax paid by each household to the see of Rome) to the Pope, in exchange for declaring Lichfield, in Mercia, an archbishop's see.

3 Of King John, who was acknowledged to have been a bad king, it was said: "foul as it is, Hell itself is made fouler by the presence of John" (Matthew Paris, Chronica 2, 669). Louis VIII was invited by the barons to become crown of England. He unsuccessfully invaded England between 1215 and 1217. Henry III, John's eldest son, succeeded him.

4 Magna Carta was signed in 1215 at Runnymede.

5 The 1733 translation is mistaken here: Voltaire wrote, "*il ôtait une plus grand tyrannie*," and the translation reads "it was a greater tyranny."

6 The Dukes of Dorset had their home at Knole, in Vert.

7 The terms "high," middle," and "low" justice have their origins in medieval times and refer to courts with different sentencing powers: "high" justice descended directly from the crown and could sentence a criminal to capital punishment. Other courts may have had local jurisdiction, or perhaps were established by authorities lower than the crown.

8 A personal tax from which the French nobility and clergy were exempt.

9 Perhaps "capitation" or poll tax.

10 William III, who seized the Stuart crown in 1688, cooperated with the establishment of the Civil List [which in effect granted the Commons control of all finance and, by and large, worked with Parliament to secure tax revenues].

Tenth Letter

1 The British have held Gibraltar since 1704. Porto-Bello is in Panama. Robinson Crusoe was one of the British sailors to have traveled there.

2 Prince Eugene of Savoy-Carignan (1663–1736) was victorious at Turin in 1706 during the War of the Spanish Succession. Voltaire's source for this letter cannot be found.

3 Charles Townshend, second Viscount Townshend (1674–1738), Secretary of State from 1714 to 1716, retired from political life to cultivate turnips.

4 Nathaniel Harley, brother of Robert (first Earl of Oxford) lived in Aleppo (Syria).

Eleventh Letter

1 Plenty of English people, and above all clerics, remained opposed to inoculation. See Anne Lacombe, "La lettre sur l'insertion de la petite vérole et *Les lettres philosophiques.*" [*Studies on Voltaire and the Eighteenth Century.* 117 (1971), 113 31.]

2 Inoculation was known as "the method of Turkey," for instance, in Edward Strother, *Dissertations upon the Ingraftment of the Small-Pox.* (London: Rivington, 1722).

3 The ruler of the Ottoman Empire.

4 The ruler of Persia, later called the Shah.

5 Voltaire mocked the Benedictines in particular for their voluminous erudition. Dom Calmet's commentary on the Old and New Testaments ran to nine volumes (1724–1726). See François Bessire, "Voltaire lecteur de Don Calmet" *Studies on Voltaire and the Eighteenth Century,* 139–77. 281 (1991).

6 Lady Mary Wortley-Montagu (bap. 1682–1762) had lost her only brother to the disease and nearly died of it herself. In Turkey she had discovered that inoculation with a live smallpox virus was a common procedure in folk medicine. With the support of Charles Maitland, she had her four-year-old son inoculated.

7 John Milton (1608–1674), author of the most famous epic poem in the English language (see Voltaire's *Essays on Epic poetry*), was estranged from his two daughters, Anne (born 1646) and Mary (born 1647) by his first wife, Anne Powell. In his will, Milton "bequeathed" an unpaid dowry of £1000 that he had never received from the father of his wife. Mindful of this story, Voltaire would, in 1763, seize the opportunity to rescue a literary descendant from poverty. In bringing Marie Louise Corneille to his home in Ferney and educating her, he thought he was restoring the dignity to the fortunes of the great playwright Pierre Corneille (1606–1684), but she in fact turned out to be the direct descendant of Thomas Corneille (1625–1709), a younger brother and lesser playwright.

8 Father Courayer (see Letter 5, note 5) was offered asylum after being chased out of France. He is buried in Westminster Abbey.

9 George II's consort, Queen Caroline of Ansbach (1683–1737), to whom Voltaire dedicated his epic poem, the *Henriade*, became interested in inoculation while Princess of Wales and arranged an experiment on prisoners in Newgate gaol. In the eyes of some people, Lady Mary became notorious for being an "unnatural mother" who had played with the lives of her children. Lady Mary Wortley Montagu, *Essays, Poems and "Simplicity: A Comedy,"* ed. R. Halsband and I. Grundy (1977); rev. edn (1993), pp. 35–36.

10 Monseigneur, the grandfather of Louis XV and son of Louis XIV, died in 1711. He was known as Monseigneur le Dauphin during his lifetime and, after his death, as le *Grand Dauphin* to distinguish him from his son.

Twelfth Letter

1 Although Voltaire claims to be tired of such debates (in which, above all, the respective accomplishments of Alexander the Great and Socrates were placed in the balance), Voltaire repeatedly expressed the wish that man would be less seduced by military glory and more impressed by constructive achievements. Voltaire, for instance, sounds this refrain in arguing for the superiority of Peter the Great (founder of St. Petersburg) over his belligerent adversary Charles XII (see the preface to his *History of Peter the Great*), while Louis XIV's promotion of the arts guarantees his enduring greatness in the eyes of Voltaire.

2 Francis Bacon (1561–1626), the son of the Lord Keeper, became attorney general and then Lord Keeper himself. In 1618, Bacon became Lord Chancellor (the most eminent lawyer in England) and, raised to the peerage, was created Baron Verulam during the reign of James I (1603–1625).

3 Bacon's character, reputation and legacy remained complicated after his life. See N. Mathews, *Francis Bacon: The History of a Character Assassination* (1996).

4 Effiat accompanied Henrietta Maria on her journey to England to become the wife of Charles I.

5 Henri IV.

6 Charles I of England.

7 Bacon was impeached for taking bribes in 1621. He was fined £40,000, imprisoned in the Tower of London, and forbidden to come within twelve miles of the court.

8 The *Novum Organum*, Bacon's major philosophical work, was published in 1620. Voltaire shared Bacon's dim view of the teaching in universities. See J. Gascoigne, *Science, Politics and Universities in Europe, 1600–1800* (Aldershot: Ashgate, 1998) and Lawrence Brockliss, *French Higher Education in the Seventeenth and Eighteenth Centuries: A Cultural History* (Oxford: Oxford University Press, 1987).

9 *A parte rei*: in reality. For the persistent interest in Aristotle's thought and the continuing respect it commanded, see E. Grant, "Aristotelianism and the Longevity of the Medieval World View," *History of Science* 16 (1978).

10 Evangelista Torricelli (1608–1647).

11 The *Maxims* of the Duc de La Rochefoucauld and the *Essays* of Montaigne were published in editions throughout the eighteenth century. Bacon's essays discussed here are *The essayes or counsels, civill and morall* (1625).

12 Bacon's *History of Henry VII* (1622) was to have been followed by a similar history of Henry VIII. Jacques-Auguste de Thou (1553–1617) was the author of the voluminous *Histoire universelle*.

13 Voltaire is referring to Perkin Warbeck (*c*.1474–1499), who claimed to be a son of Edward IV and thus heir to the throne of England.

Thirteenth Letter

1 John Locke (1632–1704) was a hero to Voltaire. His *Essay on Human Understanding* and ideas on sensationalism exerted a great influence on Voltaire and other eighteenth-century thinkers.

2 Anaxagoras, an ancient Greek thinker, discovered the true causes of eclipses.

3 Jean Mabillon (1632–1707) was a Benedictine Monk of the order of Saint Maur. He edited the works of St. Bernard.

4 These were, in order, Alexander of Hales (b. 1245, of Oxford), Duns Scotus, Saint Thomas Aquinas, Saint Bonaventure; the "Cherubic Doctor" was an invention of Rabelais in his *Pantagruel* (chapter VII).

5 The 1733 English translation translates "*la physique*" as "physics," using the term in its widest sense.

6 *Italics* added here to make the contradiction more apparent.

7 Boileau-Despréaux, poet, author of the *Art poétique* and, briefly, *Historiographe de roi*, like Voltaire.

8 Edward Stillingfleet (1635–1699), Bishop of Worcester and theologian, criticised Locke's *Essay Concerning Human Understanding* and wrote two books against Locke. Locke replied with lengthy answers of his own, finishing with *Mr. Locke's Reply to the Right Reverend the Lord Bishop of Worcester's Answer to his Second Letter* (1699).

9 Descartes' argument that animals were mechanistic would soon be taken up by eighteenth-century philosophers who went further and argued that man was no different. See L. Cohen-Rosenfeld, *From Beast Machine to Man Machine* (New York, 1968).

10 Voltaire provides an assortment of philosophers who not only did "carry dissent into their lands" but found themselves exiled from those lands. Locke lived in exile, first in France and then in the Netherlands where Pierre Bayle also lived in exile. Baruch Spinoza (1632–1677), excommunicated from his synagogue, led a reclusive existence in the Netherlands. Thomas Hobbes

(1588–1679) lived in France; Anthony Ashley Cooper, third Earl of Shaftesbury (1671–1713) wrote *Characteristicks of Men, Manners, Opinions, Times* (1711); a friend of Locke, Anthony Collins was the author of *An Historical and Critical Essay on the 39 Articles of the Church of England* (1724); John Toland (1670–1722) wrote *Christianity not Mysterious* (1695). His habit of conducting theological debates in taverns made him a notorious figure, while his doubts about beliefs and dogmas that were dangerous to challenge attracted controversy.

Fourteenth Letter

[1] Cartesians, or followers of Descartes, sometimes said to be more Cartesian than Descartes himself had been.

[2] *Non nostrum inter vos tantas componere lites.* [It is not for us to judge in such great matters.]

[3] A eulogy of Newton by Bernard le Bovier Fontenelle (1657–1757) was published in 1727. Newton's membership (as a foreign associate) of the Académie royale des sciences brought with it the obligation on the part of the Académie to mark his death with an *éloge*.

[4] Descartes took up an invitation to live at the court of Queen Christina in Sweden, where he is supposed to have died on account of the cold.

[5] Descartes, who fought in the Thirty Years War (1618–1648), explains in the beginning of his *Discourse on Method* that all his experiences of life have told him nothing about the truth.

[6] Galileo (1564–1642) is supposed to have lived under house arrest rather than to have languished in prison. See Rivera Feldhay, *Galileo and the Church: Political Inquisition or Critical Dialogue?* (Cambridge: Cambridge University Press, 1995).

[7] Francis van Schooten (1615–1660), who dedicated a work to Descartes and Pierre Fermat (1601–1665).

[8] Jacques Rohault (1620–1675), author of the *Traité de physique* (1671).

Fifteenth Letter

[1] This sentence is almost a direct quotation from Henry Pemberton's *A View of Sir Isaac Newton's Philosophy* (London, printed by S. Palmer, 1728), Book II, Chapter 1, p. 167.

[2] Newton is thought to have returned to his birthplace at Woolsthorpe, Lincolnshire. The story of Newton's "fruit" or "apple" was first revealed in Voltaire's *An Essay on Epick Poetry* (1727). D. McKie and G. R. De Beer, "Newton's apple," *Notes and Records of the Royal Society*, 9 (1951–1952), 46–54, 333–5.

[3] Jean Picard (1620–1682), French astronomer, who increased the accuracy of astronomical obervations.

4 Parisian feet (or *pieds de roi*, 0.324 metres) appear to be somewhat larger than those in London (measuring 0.305 metres).

5 By "weighing" on the earth and sun, Voltaire means that the earth and moon "exert a gravitational attraction."

6 Edmund Halley (1656–1742) calculated that the comet that was to be named after him had a period of seventy-six years. He predicted correctly that it would return in 1758. A comet had appeared in 44 BCE, seven days after the assassination of Julius Caesar, prompting symbolic interpretations. Halley worked out from his understanding of the tides where Caesar must have landed when he invaded England.

7 Voltaire writes "Wilston" in the original French version. He perhaps is conflating Thomas Woolston (bap. 1668–1733), the religious controversialist, and William Whiston (1667–1752), a natural philosopher and Newtonian, author of *A New Theory of the Earth* (1696).

8 Joseph Saurin (1659–1737) made contributions to the calculus. Bernard Le Bovier Fontenelle (1657–1757) popularized Descartes and praised Newton. He was elected to the Royal Society in 1737.

9 *Procedes huc et non ibis amplius.* "Thus far mayest thou go, and no farther." Voltaire misquotes Job 38: 11.

Sixteenth Letter

1 René Descartes' *La Dioptrique* was published in 1637.

2 Marco Antonio de Dominis (1560–1624) made telling contributions to the science of optics during his academic career. His *De Radiis Visus et Lucis*, published in Venice in 1611, analysed the refractions of light in droplets of water. See Noel Malcolm, *De Dominis (1560–1624): Venetian, Anglican, Ecumenist, and Relapsed Heretic* (London: Strickland & Scott, 1984).

Seventeenth Letter

1 John Wallis (1616–1703) was a cryptographer and mathematician. Voltaire appears to be alluding to his *Arithmetica Infinitorum*, which was first published in 1655. Wallis found an infinite series expressing the value of $4/\pi$ by a series of interpolations. The very term for the method was coined by Wallis, whose techniques in this work seemed to be similar to those he used in deciphering coded letters.

2 William Brouncker, second Viscount of Lyons (1620–1684). Like Wallis, a founder of the Royal Society (1660). He first expressed the ratio of the area of a circle to the circumscribed square as an infinite continued fraction.

3 Nicolaus Mercator (*c.*1620–1687) This would appear to be his study on the motion of planets, *Hypothesis Astronomica Nova* (1664). He was not related to Gerardus Mercator, although he too was interested in map projection.

4 A differential calculus in its simplest form gives a rigorous definition for a concept—the rate of change. Integral calculus is motivated by the wish to formalize intuitive ideas of the definition of the area enclosed by an arbitrary closed curve.

5 The third and last volume of Wallis' *Opera Mathematica* (1693–1699) contained a collection of letters on the priority dispute between Newton and Leibniz. See A. Rupert Hall, *Philosophers at War: The Quarrel Between Newton and Leibniz* (Cambridge: Cambridge University Press, 1980) and D. Bertoloni Meli, *Equivalence and Priority: Newton versus Leibniz* (Cambridge: Cambridge University Press, 1993). Johan Bernoulli (1667–1748) not only contested Newton's discovery but expropriated the ideas of his son, Daniel.

6 The circulation of blood discovered by William Harvey (1578–1657) was vigorously contested by the French anatomist, Jean Riolan (1580–1657) who, however, claimed as his own a different, reduced sense of circulation.

7 The discovery by Claude Perrault (1613–1688) of the circulation of sap was the source of another Anglo-French controversy. Voltaire may have in mind the horticulturist Ralph Austen, (*c.*1612–1676).

8 Nicolas Hartsoeker (1656–1725) postulated that worms develop in the intestines. Anton van Leeuwenhoek (1632–1723), who improved and refined the microscope, saw these worms. Hartsoeker was the pupil of Christiaan Huygens (1629–1695).

9 The problem of the cycloid, the arc traced by a point on the circumference of a traveling wheel, was proposed by Blaise Pascal. Christopher Wren (1632–1723) partially solved the problem, but Pascal was not convinced.

10 Voltaire refers to Newton's *The Chronology of Ancient Kingdoms Amended* (1728) from which the discussion that follows is drawn.

11 Founder of the city of Memphis, Menes (also known as Aha) was the founding king of the first dynasty. Sethon, according to Herodotus, reigned 11,340 years after him.

12 The Olympiad was the unit of a chronological era in ancient Greece, corresponding to four years. The first is supposed to have occurred in 776 BCE.

13 Colure is one of two great circles intersecting at right angles in the poles of the equator.

14 The 1733 translation renders Voltaire's "*figure*" as "figure." Voltaire may be referring to the discussions of whether the earth's sphere is true or flattened.

15 The Peloponnesian War (431 BCE–404 BCE) was contested by Athens and the Peloponnesian League, led by Sparta, and memorably recounted by Thucydides.

Eighteenth Letter

[1] In the sixteenth century there was only one permanent theatre in Paris, that on the site of the Hôtel de Bourgogne, leased to professional actors from 1578. Theatres in England were older. See Janette Dillon, *The Cambridge Introduction to Early English Theatre* (Cambridge: Cambridge University Press, 2006). See Margaret Greer, "The development of national theater" in *The Cambridge History of Spanish Literature* (Cambridge: Cambridge University Press, 2004).

[2] Shakespeare (1564–1616) was a contemporary of Lope de Vega (1562–1635). Pierre Corneille (1606–1684) was not considered the "French Shakespeare" to the extent that Shakespeare later would be called the "English Corneille."

[3] Voltaire was not alone in flinching at the coarseness of some of the action in Shakespeare. Already the diarist John Evelyn (1620–1706) remarked that "these old plays begin to disgust this refined age" E.L. Avery and others, *The London Stage, 1660–1800*, (Carbondale, IL: Southern Illinois University Press, 1960) 11 vols., I. 43. Moreover, plays like *Othello*, performed in 1660, once Charles II was restored to the throne and reopened theaters (and possibly featuring for the first time ever a woman playing a woman's part), were cut to suit the more delicate tastes of the eighteenth century. Unlike many of Shakespeare's other plays, *Hamlet* did not suffer from radical cutting after the Restoration. Nor did *Julius Caesar*, although it was not staged between 1780 and 1812 for fear that it might encourage a French Revolution in England.

[4] *Venice Preserv'd*, first staged in February 1682, was the most famous play by Thomas Otway (1632–1685). The scenes between Aquilina and Antonio were, as Voltaire suggests, rapidly excised from productions and publications of *Venice Preserv'd*. In his "Life of Otway," Samuel Johnson regretted the "despicable scenes of vile comedy" in *Venice Preserv'd*, but he also observed that the "striking passages are in every mouth." (Johnson, *Lives of the English Poets*, (1780–1781).

[5] The modern English translation of Voltaire's French is provided here, as an additional point of reference:

> To be or not to be, that is the question.
> To stay: one must choose, either instantly to move
> From life to death, from being to nothingness.
> Cruel gods! If it be so, illuminate my courage.
> Must I grow old bent under this hand that insults me,
> Endure or end my misery and my fate?
> Who am I? Who stops me? And what is death?
> It is the end of our troubles, my only refuge;
> After long agonies, a quiet sleep;
> We go to sleep, and all dies. But a dreadful awakening
> May perhaps succeed the sweetness of sleep.

We are threatened, told that this short life
Is quickly followed by eternal torment.
O death! Fatal moment! Dreadful eternity!
Every heart freezes in horror at thy very name.
Eh! Who without thee could bear this life,
Who could bless the hypocrisy of our lying priests?
Or praise the faults of an unworthy mistress?
Crawl beneath a lord, worship his haughtiness,
And show the despair of one's defeated soul
To ungrateful friends who look away?
Death would be too sweet in such extremities;
But scruples speak and cry out, "Stop."
They restrain our hands from this blessed homicide,
And change a warrior hero into a timid Christian, etc.

6 Voltaire echoes the sentiments of John Dryden (1631–1700), who in the dedication attached to the play *Aureng-Zebe* (staged November 17, 1675, printed 1676), described himself as "the *Sisyphus* of the Stage." The lines quoted are drawn from Act IV, Scene I.

7 This passage comes from John Dryden's play *Aureng Zebe*.

8 *Cato* by Joseph Addison (1672–1719) was premiered at Drury Lane on 14 April 1713, and immediately became a great success as rival parties sought to appropriate to their cause all the beautiful verse and elegant sentiments mentioned by Voltaire.

9 *Pompey*, by Pierre Corneille, first performed in 1643, featured a character named Cornélie or Cornelia. Voltaire frequently and favorably compared young Marie Louise, the descendant of Corneille whom he adopted, to this character. Voltaire himself endeavoured to show that it was possible and indeed preferable, even for a Frenchman, to write a tragedy without love. *Rome sauvée ou Catilina* (1752) was offered explicitly as proof of this. *Mérope* (1737) offered perhaps Voltaire's most successful example of the genre.

10 Marly or Marly le Roi was a retreat built for Louis XIV, supposedly to offer him peace and respite from courtiers, although it apparently cost more than Versailles [Saint Simon, *Mémoires*, ed. Gonzague Truc (Paris: Gallinard, 1953) 7 vols., iv, 1009]. It is surprising that Voltaire should choose Marly as the French counterpoint to the freer English picturesque garden, because it exemplified relative informality in French garden design.

Nineteenth Letter

1 Béat Louis (or Ludwig) de Muralt (1665–1749), a Swiss visitor to England, published his *Letters on the English and the French* in 1725, a somewhat frivolous forerunner of Voltaire's *Philosophical Letters*.

2 Voltaire's assessment of the comedies of Thomas Shadwell (c.1640–1692) chimes with critical opinion, formed in part by the satirical portrayal of Shadwell as a foolish hack in Dryden's play, *MacFlecknoe* (published in 1682).

3 Contemporary English translations attribute this statement to Voltaire and prefer "*of which it might be said*" to "*of which it has been said.*"

4 William Wycherley (bap. 1641–1716) was the lover of Barbara Villiers (bap. 1640–1709), a "woman of great beauty but most enormously vicious and ravenous; foolish but imperious" according to Bishop Burnet [Burnet *History of His Own Time* (Edinburgh: Hamilton, Balfour & Neill, 1753) 5 vols., I, 132]. She had been the mistress of Charles II, by whom she had three or four children. She also had affairs with Jacob Hall, the rope-dancer, and the Duke of Marlborough.

5 Wycherley's *Plain Dealer*, first performed in 1676, was written in imitation of *The Misanthrope* (1666) by Molière. Wycherley henceforward became known himself as the Plain-Dealer or Manly, the character's surname, although that role was played by the actor Charles Hart. Barbara Villiers had an affair with him too.

6 Wycherley's *The Country-Wife*, performed in 1676. Molière's *School for Wives* was written in 1662.

7 The battle of Hochstaedt (1704), known in English as the Battle of Blenheim. The victorious general, the Duke of Marlborough, was rewarded with Blenheim Palace, designed by Sir John Vanbrugh (1664–1726). Its dramatic skyline and gargantuan scale shocked some eighteenth-century sensibilities.

8 Voltaire's French does not capture the rhyme in Vanbrugh's epitaph— "Under this stone, reader, survey / Dead Sir John Vanbrugh's house of clay. / Lie heavy on him, Earth! For he / Laid many heavy loads on thee."—Vanbrugh was buried in St. Stephen Walbrook, London. No record remains of the grave stone, said to be inscribed by his fellow architect, Nicholas Hawksmoor.

9 Vanbrugh was caught up in an elaborate spy-swapping controversy and imprisoned in the Bastille around 1692. It is not clear which, if any, of Vanbrugh's comedies was written in the Bastille, but the prison was, as Voltaire found, comparatively comfortable. Thus not only did Vanbrugh refrain from criticizing his captors, but his "love for France was increased, strangely enough, by his captivity." Introduction to *The Relapse* (London: Peter Nevill, 1948), p. 5.

10 In his last poem, William Congreve (1670–1729) portrays himself as "not so robust in body, as in mind / and always undejected, tho' declined" (*The Complete Works of Congreve*, ed. by E. Davis (Chicago: Chicago University Press, 1967). His eyesight was failing; he had gout, and probably by the time Voltaire visited, he had endured an accident in his carriage. Voltaire no doubt regretted the "fault" he identifies. In the Amsterdam edition of 1738–1739, he excised the passage critical of Congreve.

11 Jean-Baptiste de Lully (1632–1687), known as the "father of opera." Giovanni Battista Bononcini (1670–1747) admired Lully, as well having a first name in common.

12 It is difficult to see how the physician, Richard Mead (1673–1754), came to admire Claude–Adrien Helvétius (1715–1777), himself from a family of physicians, since his most important works date from later in the century. But Jean-Batiste Silva already had a reputation as an eminent physician and published *Le traité de l'usage des différentes sortes de saignées principalement de celle du pied* in 1727.

13 Sir Richard Steele (bap. 1672–1729) is better known as an essayist but wrote poetry, while Colley Cibber (1671–1757), who was appointed Poet Laureate in 1730, was chiefly a playwright. Whether they wrote in verse or prose, playwrights were often designated as "poets," and indeed previous poets laureate, like Shadwell, were playwrights.

14 Plautus (*c*.254 BCE–184 BCE), the author of comedies like *Amphitryon* (which provided the subject for a tragedy by Sophocles) and Aristophanes (*c*.446–*c*.388 BCE), author of *The Birds* and *The Frogs* among others. Voltaire's rival and contemporary Jean-Jacques Rousseau, argues similarly (in his *Lettre à d'Alembert sur les spectacles*) that tragedy owes less than comedy to the social conventions of the country in which it is written.

Twentieth Letter

1 Deloffre points out that Voltaire's original French text read, "*qu'ils ne sont ici en France*," a slip on Voltaire's part indicating that the letter was written in France, not in England.

2 John Wilmot, second Earl of Rochester (1647–1680), spent his early life in Paris, with his exiled family. Guillaume Amfrye de Chaulieu (1639–1720), Jean-François Sarrazin (1611?–1654) and Claude-Emmanuel Luillier Chapelle (1626–1686) were known for their poetic elegance.

3 Deloffre identifies him as John Hervey, second Baron of Ickworth (1696–1743). Hervey's original text in English appears at the end of this letter.

4 Voltaire met Hervey in England. Voltaire would therefore have been able to verify Lady Wortley Montagu's observation that the world consisted of "men, women and Herveys."

5 Voltaire's footnote: "He no doubt refers to the farces that some preachers enact in public places."

6 Deloffre cites John Hervey, *The Note Books of John Hervey*, edited by Besterman (1968); the spelling and punctuation are as they appear in Deloffre's text.

7 A modern translation of Voltaire's French has been supplied as an additional point of reference:

What then did I see in Italy?
Pride, cunning, and poverty.
Great compliments, little kindness,
And much ceremony.
The extravagant comedy
That the Inquisition often
Calls religion,
But that we call folly.
Nature, beneficent in vain,
Wishes to enrich these lovely places;
But the devastating hand of priests
Stifles the best of its gifts.
Monseigneurs, the self-designated great,
Alone in their magnificent palaces,
Are elegant do-nothings,
Penniless and servantless.
As for the lower priests, without liberty,
Martyrs under the oppressive yoke,
They have taken an oath of poverty,
Praying to God out of laziness,
Fasting, because of famine.
These beautiful places, blessed by the Pope,
Seem inhabited by devils,
And the miserable inhabitants
Are damned in paradise.

Twenty-First Letter

[1] Rochester's reputation as a libertine was well established in his own lifetime. Saint-Evremond (bap. 1614–1703), who had spent some time in the Bastille, wrote *Memoirs of Rochester*, published in 1709.

[2] Voltaire's original French translation, in classical rhymed hexameter couplets, appears on p. 84.

[3] Deloffre points out that the first dozen lines represent Voltaire's radical compression of much of Rochester's poem. For the most part, the rest of the lines correspond to the original. Rochester's verses (omitted from Voltaire's translation), as cited by Deloffre, follow:

> . . . This busy puzzling stirrer up of doubt
> That frames deep mysteries, then finds 'em out:
> Filling, with frantic crowds of thinking fools,
> These rev'rend Bedlams, colleges and schools;
> Borne on those wings, each heavy sot can pierce

The limits of the boundless universe . . .

And we have modern cloister'd coxcombs, who
Retire to think, 'cause they have nought to do:
But thoughts are given for action's government;
Where action ceases, thought's impertinent.
Our sphere of action is life's happiness;
And he who thinks beyond, thinks like an ass.

4 Edmund Waller (1606–1687), widely read in the eighteenth century, wrote poetry in praise of both Cromwell and Charles II. He was well known in France, where he lived in exile from 1644 to 1652. Jean de La Fontaine (1621–1695), best known for his fables from the seventeenth century, but also the author of stories popular in the eighteenth century, praised Waller in a letter addressed to M. de Bonrepaux in London [*Oeuvres diverses* (Paris: Gallinard, 1948) p. 165]. Pierre Bayle (1647–1706), who lived in exile in the Netherlands, compiled the highly influential *Dictionnaire historique et critique* (1697, enlarged in 1702) in which he refers to Waller.

5 Vincent Voiture (1598–1648), renowned for his light wit, was one of the circle that met at the Hôtel de Rambouillet, a center of intellectual life in the first half of the seventeenth century. He was, according to Voltaire, the first "bel esprit" (or "fine wit") in France (*Oeuvres historiques*, p. 1213). He occupied the seat (number 33) in the Académie française to which Voltaire would eventually be elected.

6 Jean Regnault de Segrais (1625–1701) translated Virgil into French verse. Voltaire repeats the assertion that nobody reads it in his *Siècle de Louis XIV*.

7 Voltaire felt that Philippe Quinault (1635–1688) was underestimated, in part because people thought he owed his reputation to Lully who set his verse to music (*Oeuvres historiques*, p. 1995).

8 Jean de La Fontaine, poet and author of the *Fables*.

9 Cromwell died during severe storms in 1658. Richard Mead regarded this as an act of Providence in *De imperio solis ac lunae in corpora humana et morbis inde veniendis* (*On the Influence of the Sun and Moon on Human Bodies and the Diseases Arising Thence*), published in 1704. Waller's eulogy of Cromwell is more likely to have been the "Panegyrick to my Lord Protector" (1655) which was followed by "To the King, upon his Majesties Happy Return" (1660).

10 The English poem by Waller, which appeared in the English translation of 1733, appears at the end of this letter.

11 Waller was born in Coleshill, Buckinghamshire. He was wealthy, even after being fined £10,000 before his exile.

12 Voltaire's assortment of aristocratic writers consists of: Charles Sackville, sixth Earl of Dorset (1643–1706), a poet whose work circulated in manuscript form; Wentworth Dillon, fourth Earl of Roscommon (1637–1685) who was also a poet. John Sheffield, first Duke of Buckingham and

Normanby (1647–1721), sometimes known as the Duke of Buckinghamshire, refashioned Shakespeare's *Julius Caesar* to suit eighteenth-century tastes and wrote essays and verse besides. George Villiers, second Duke of Buckingham (1628–1687) wrote, among other works, a satirical play *The Rehearsal*, published five times in his own lifetime. During his lifetime, George Savile, the first Marquess of Halifax (1633–1695) was better known as a politician than as a writer.

Twenty-Second Letter

1 Matthew Prior (1664–1721) was a poet who moved between France and England as a diplomat, negotiating the terms that would result in the Treaty of Utrecht, which ended Anglo-French hostilities in the War of the Spanish Succession.

2 *Hudibras*, by Samuel Butler (bap. 1613–1680). *Hudibras*, which came out in two parts, was a great success. Butler, like Prior, travelled to France in a diplomatic party. There was, as Voltaire suggests, considerable debate as to the precise identity of the satirical targets in his poem.

3 *Don Quixote*, the masterpiece of Miguel de Cervantes (1547–1616), first published in 1605 and admired by Voltaire who thought that no Spanish literature written after *Don Quixote* was worth reading. Voltaire's *Notebooks*, ed. by Theodore Besterman (Geneva: Voltaire Foundation, 1952), 2 vols, II, 429. *Menippean Satire* (a name derived from the satirist Menippus of Gadara, third century BCE) was written by Jean Leroy and others. Published in 1594, it attacked the Catholic Ligue in favour of Protestant claims.

4 Jonathan Swift (1667–1745), the Dean of St. Patrick's Cathedral Dublin, author of *Gulliver's Travels* (or *Travels into Several Remote Nations of the World*) first appeared in 1726 and was greatly admired by Voltaire. Swift shared a reputation for coarseness with François de Rabelais (*c.*1494–*c.*1553) whose "incomprehensible book" is divided into four parts: *Pantagruel* (1532); *Gargantua* (1534); the *Tiers livre* (1546); the *Quart livre* (1548). In later years, Voltaire changed his mind about Rabelais.

5 Alexander Pope (1688–1741), whom Voltaire visited in Twickenham, on the outskirts of London. Voltaire and Pope admired one another at least until Voltaire supposedly offended Pope's mother with remarks about his misadventures at the hands of the Jesuits who taught him.

6 Voltaire mentions Pope's *Essay on Criticism* in a letter dated 1726. He seems to have encouraged the abbé du Resnel (1694–1761) to translate it into French verse, a translation published in 1730 and republished under the title, *La principes de la morale et du goût* (Paris, 1737).

7 Pope first published the comic poem, the *Rape of the Lock* in 1712. Voltaire quotes verses from iv.13–36.

8 A translation in modern English has been provided as an additional point of reference:

Instantly Umbriel, the old surly gnome,
Goes off, with a heavy wing and a sour look,
To find, grumbling, the deep cavern
Where, far from the soft rays spread by the eye of the world,
The goddess of mists chose her abode.
The bitter north winds whistle at the entrance,
And the unhealthy breeze of their dry breath
Brings to the place fever and headache.
On a rich sofa, sheltered by a screen,
Far from torches, noise, jabberers, and wind,
The capricious goddess continually rests,
Her heart full of sorrows that have no cause,
Never thinking, her mind always troubled,
Her eye heavy, her complexion pale, her spleen engorged.
Malicious Envy sits next to her,
An old ghost-like witch, a withered virgin,
With the air of piety destroying her neighbor,
Slandering the world, Bible in hand.
Carelessly reclining on a flowery bed,
A young beauty rests near her:
It is Affectation, who lisps as she speaks,
Listens without hearing, squints as she looks,
Blushes without shame, laughs without joy,
Pretends she is prey to a hundred maladies,
And full of health, under her rouge and powder,
Softly complains, and artfully faints.

9 *Le Lutrin* by Boileau, a heroic-comic poem first published in 1674, which revolves around the placement of a lectern. Personified Apathy (*mollesse* in French) makes an appearance in the second canto.

10 Blaise Pascal (1623–1662) satirized the Jesuits in his *Lettres provinciales* (1656–1657). The Jansenists, of whom Pascal was probably the most eloquent representative, were not alone in thinking that the sermons of the Jesuit Louis Bourdaloue (1632–1704) were too long. Such was his verbosity that he is supposed to have lent his name to a portable urinal, carried into church.

11 The execution of Mary Stuart (Mary I of Scotland or Mary Queen of Scots), consort of François II, polarized opinion in the eighteenth century. She was regarded variously as a martyr to the Catholic faith and a sexually transgressive traitoress. Later, Schiller's play *Maria Stuart* (1800) and Sir Walter Scott's novel *The Abbot* (1820) helped to romanticise her story.

12 Thomas Gordon (d.1750), a radical journalist who translated Tacitus' works in four volumes prefixing them with *Political Discourses on that Author* (London: Woodward & Peele, 1737).

13 Paul de Rapin de Thoyras (1661–1725), a French Protestant who fled to England after the revocation of the Edict of Nantes. Rapin had tried to explain the party system in Britain in his *Dissertation sur les whigs et les tories* (The Hague, 1717), before proceeding to publish the first eight volumes of his *Histoire d'Angleterre* in 1723.

Twenty-Third Letter

1 Voltaire is alluding to the seventeenth-century foundations, the Académie française (1635), the Académie royale de peinture et sculpture (1648), Académie des inscriptions et belles-lettres (1663), Académie royale des sciences (1666), the Académie royale d'architecture (1671). All were suppressed in 1793.

2 King Charles II founded the Royal Observatory in 1675, with the hope of solving the problem of finding longitude at sea. In 1714, the British Government offered, by Act of Parliament, a prize of £20,000 for a solution which could provide longitude to within half-a-degree (two minutes of time). A Board of Longitude was set up to act as judges. Many people, including, it seems, Voltaire, believed that the problem simply could not be solved. Indeed, the phrase "finding the longitude" became a sort of catchphrase for the pursuits of fools and madmen. The "impossible" longitude problem was eventually solved by John Harrison (1693–1776), a joiner from Lincolnshire with little formal education. He received the prize in 1773, but not before being treated with great suspicion and being subjected to a trial.

3 Addison was made under-secretary in the office of the secretary of state for the southern department in 1706. Two years later, he was then appointed secretary to the new Lord Lieutenant of Ireland.

4 Newton served as Warden and then as Master of the Mint, responsible for coinage in Great Britain. Voltaire mischievously suggested that Newton owed this position to his niece, Catherine Barton, whom Voltaire met, but Newton was one of a committee called in to address problems of coinage caused, in part, by counterfeiters and clippers (those who clipped the edges of coins without a definite rim).

5 Congreve was, at different times, one of the commissioners for regulating and licensing hackney coaches, customs collector at Poole, a commissioner for wine licences, undersearcher of the London port and, after 1714, secretary of Jamaica.

6 Swift became Dean of St Patrick's Cathedral, Dublin in 1713. The Primate of Ireland and Archbishop of Dublin at that time was William King (1650–1729).

7 Just as Newton's refusal to subscribe to the articles of the Church of England put his career at risk in Cambridge, so Pope's Catholicism excluded him from public office and required him to live outside the center of

London. The figure cited by Voltaire that Pope's translations of Homer's *Iliad* and *Odyssey* earned him has been considered accurate. See David Foxon, *Pope and the Early Eighteenth-Century Book Trade*, revised and edited by James McLaverty (Oxford: Clarendon, 1991).

8 Prosper Jolyot de Crébillon, or Crébillon *père* (1674–1762) was the author of *Rhadamiste et Zénobie*. The story of his poverty was well known, as was the fact that he wrote large parts of his works in his head. Voltaire and Crébillon were later to become bitter rivals as playwrights.

9 The benefactor appears to be Guy-Crescent Fagon (1638–1718), a botanist of some repute who helped Louis Racine (1692–1763), the son of the great Jean Racine and a poet himself, secure an administrative post.

10 Pope had been painted by Sir Godfrey Kneller and Charles Jervas by the time Voltaire was in England. See William K. Wimsatt, *The Portraits of Alexander Pope* (New Haven: Yale University Press, 1965).

11 The body of Newton lay in state before being interred in Westminster Abbey in 1727. The Lord Chancellor was among the aristocrats who bore the pall.

12 Anne Oldfield (1683–1730), who played the role of Cato's daughter in Addison's play before she became pregnant.

13 Adrienne Lecouvreur (1692–1730) died in the same year as Oldfield, but as an actress, she was refused a Christian burial. Voltaire expressed his fury in a poem, *Sur la mort d'Adrienne Lecouvreur*, that was offered as a compensatory monument, an alternative "Saint Denis." The Basilica of Saint Denis contained a great number of French royal tombs.

14 Charles I and his consort, Henrietta Maria, daughter of Henry IV of France.

15 In a pamphlet against stage plays, *Histriomastix* (1633), William Prynne (1600–1669) denounced female actors. Unfortunately, Queen Henrietta Maria was participating in a court masque at the same time. Prynne was tried and found guilty. At first, in 1633, his ears were only slightly cropped, but later they were chopped off; his nose was slit, and the initials "S. L." (for "Seditious Libeller") were burnt into his cheeks.

16 Voltaire takes a delight in summarizing the flagrant errors and anachronisms he perceives in (or attributes to) Prynne and particularly enjoys relating these details, having himself written a play entitled *Oedipus* (1718).

17 Senesino (1686–1758), a famous castrato present in London at roughly the same time as London. Francesca Cuzzoni (1700–1770) was an Italian soprano, who also performed in London. Voltaire, like Candide, is rather dismayed by *castrati* singing the parts of heroes, like Julius Caesar.

18 Pierre Le Brun wrote a *Discours sur la comédie, où l'on voit la réponse au théologien qui la défend* (1694, reprinted 1731).

Twenty-Fourth Letter

1 The Royal Society (or, to give its full name, Royal Society of London for the Improvement of Natural Knowledge) was founded in 1660.

2 Voltaire no doubt exaggerates the contrast between French and English academies, for in 1731 a rule was introduced, requiring each candidate for election to be proposed in writing. See Margery Purver, *The Royal Society: Concept and Creation* (London: Routledge, 1967). Perhaps Voltaire already suspected that it would take him three attempts to enter the Académie française, which admitted him nearly three years after he was elected to the Royal Society on November 3, 1743. Nevertheless, Fellows of the Royal Society were expected to pay, while their French counterparts were remunerated but also expected to be useful to the state. See Robin Briggs, "The Académie royale des sciences and the Pursuit of Utility," *Past and Present*, 131 (1991), 38–87.

3 In 1699, Newton was elected to the Académie royale des sciences as one of its eight foreign associates.

4 Swift's project to find an English answer to the French Academy took shape in *A Proposal for Correcting, Improving and Ascertaining the English Tongue* (1712). Its purpose was to establish "a society or academy for correcting and settling our language, that we may not perpetually be changing as we do." But when Queen Anne died unexpectedly in 1714, Swift's hopes were dashed and he left for Ireland. The British Academy was not founded until 1902.

5 Jean Chapelain (1595–1674) was the author of the laborious, incomplete, maligned epic poem, *La Pucelle* (Voltaire wrote a mock-epic poem on the same subject); Guillaume Colletet (1598–1659) wrote about the lives of the poets, but the manuscripts were partly lost in the fires that destroyed the Louvre during the *Commune* (1870); Charles Cotin (1604–1682) enjoyed the distinction of being ridiculed by both Boileau and Molière; Jacques Cassagne (1636–1679) has been said to have died prematurely as a result of Boileau's satirical attentions; Nicolas Faret (1600–1646) composed an ode to Richelieu, the founder of the Académie (in 1635) but did not live much longer; poor Perrin has been completely forgotten by the Académie française.

6 Cardinal de Richelieu (1585–1642) was the founder of the Académie and its first "Protector." When he died, the Chancellor Pierre Séguier (1588–1672) took the responsibility, which, upon his death, in turn was passed on to Louis XIV.

7 *Vitium est temporis potius quam hominis* (Seneca, d. 65CE)

8 These eulogies remain prescribed. See Michael Hawcroft, *Rhetoric: Readings in French Literature* (Oxford: Oxford University Press, 1999, pp. 65–78) for a discussion of the strategies employed by a more recent academician, Marguerite Yourcenar, to avoid boring the public.

9 Henri Morin published "Des privilèges de la main droite," *Mémoires de l'académie des inscriptions et belles-lettres* (1723), III, 68–72. Voltaire himself appears to have been right-handed.

10 Huygens took part in lengthy discussions with Bernard Renau d'Elisagaray (1652–1719) who wrote a treaty on the maneuvering of ships and was a pioneer in the armament of ships with bombs, hoping to try them out against Algerians. See Fontenelle's *Eloge, histoire de l'académie royale des sciences* (1719), pp. 101–20.

11 Jacques Coeur (*c*.1395–1456), a famous and rich merchant. Delmet appears to be Sir Peter Delmé (d. 1728), who was Governor of the Bank of England and suitably wealthy.

12 Voltaire is alluding to the abbé de Rothelin (1691–1744), with whom he corresponded. Voltaire would later, in 1764, take it upon himself to publish Pierre Corneille's works in his *Commentaires sur Corneille*, which, under the auspices of the Académie française, commented and corrected detail in his plays.

Twenty-Fifth Letter

1 The exact reasons for Voltaire's inclusion of considerations on Pascal (1623–1662) within a volume about England are unclear, as is the date of their composition. Pascal never traveled to England. But his *Pensées* had been translated into English in 1704. Voltaire takes the view, shared by some Pascal scholars, that he died before he could write them up properly, wishing to leave them in their fragmentary state.

2 He may be thinking of King Jehoiakim, who burned the prophecies of Jeremiah (cf. Jeremiah 36).

3 Deloffre points out that Pascal, in his manuscript, crossed out "where he is." Voltaire may have used one of the printed versions of the *Pensées* edited by Pascal's nephew Etienne Périer.

4 Voltaire not only asserts that there were laws of Minos but will go further and write a tragedy in five acts entitled *Les lois de Minos ou Astérie* (1773). Hesiod is thought to have lived around 700 BCE, perhaps at the same time as Homer, it is thought.

5 The Battle of Ramillies (1706), another victory for the Duke of Marlborough's troops after the success of Hochstaedt (or Blenheim) in 1704, spelled disaster for the French. The battle of Denain (1712), also in the War of the Spanish Succession, was, however, won by the French.

6 The Decalogue, or Ten Commandments, were presented to Moses on Mount Sinai.

7 Luis Molina (1535–1600), a Spanish Jesuit who held that free will could be reconciled with God's omniscience. Such views were anathema to Jansenists like Pascal.

8 When Voltaire moves to his estate at Ferney, as if to vindicate this view of man, he becomes, in his own words "the planter of cabbages and the sower of grain" (*Le planteur de choux et le semeur de grains*) (D8806, 1760).

9 Voltaire's belief in the vital necessity of action extends to and sanctions his own vocation as writer. "I write in order to act" (*j'écris pour agir'*), he writes on April 25, 1767 (as opposed to Rousseau who merely "writes in order to write").

10 Cinéas, from Thessaly, was a friend of Pyrrhus, King of Epirus. Cinéas was despatched to declare war on Rome but persuaded him not to enter hostilities.

11 Michel de Montaigne (1533–1592) wrote extensively about himself in his *Essais*, memorably providing details of the kidney stones from which he suffered. See Charles R. Mack, "Montaigne in Italy: Of Kidney Stones and Thermal Spas," *Renaissance Papers* (1991), 105–24.

12 The three-volume *Historia Coelestis Britannica*, a catalogue of all the fixed stars visible from Britain, compiled by John Flamsteed (1646–1719) was published in 1725. The stars were all enumerated with so-called Flamsteed numbers.

13 Pierre Nicole (1625–1695), a brilliant Jansenist in the circle of Pascal.

14 "A ferocious people believe that life is nothing without weapons."

15 The Marshal de Villars (1653–1734) was a brilliant general who distinguished himself in the reign of Louis XIV, despite losing to Marlborough at Malplaquet. Voltaire, in the third canto of his mock-epic poem *La Pucelle*, sang of *l'heureux Villars, fanfaron plein de cœur*—a braggart full of heart.

16 Horace (Epistle I, 1, lines 28–29): *Non possis oculo quantum contendere Lynceus, / Non tamen idcirco contemnas lippus inungi.*

Proposal for a letter about the English

1 John Dennis' "portrait" of the French is painted in his *Miscellanies in Verse and Prose* (London: Knapton, 1693). He was an unrelenting critic of Alexander Pope, who satirized him in turn in his *Dunciad*. See H.G. Paul, *John Dennis: His Life and Criticism*. (New York: Columbia University Press, 1931).

2 Elis, a city-state near Olympia in ancient Greece, was famous for horse-breeding.

3 Voltaire writes *"un combat de gladiateurs."*

4 The *Quadrille* was a card game for four people. It also lent its name to a dance, once performed on horseback.

5 The physician seems to be paraphrasing a nursery rhyme: "When the wind is in the east / 'Tis good for neither man nor beast."

6 Voltaire thought the Duke of Marlborough (1650–1722), victor of Blenheim, "The man the most fatal to the grandeur of France that had been

seen for centuries." (*Siècle de Louis XIV, Oeuvres historiques*, p.821). Voltaire is probably alluding to remarks made in the House of Lords by the Duke of Bolton (Charles Poulet, 1661–1722) that nearly prompted a duel between the two gentlemen. See *Journal of the House of Lords*, vol. 19: 1709–1714 (1802), pp. 460–61 (28 May, 1712).

7 Probably another allusion to John Dennis or, once again, Edmund Curll whose notorious biographies were "one of the new terrors of death" (Robert Carruthers, *The Poetical Works of Alexander Pope*. (London: Ingram, Cooke, 1853). 4 vols., vol.1, ch.3.

8 The unfortunate fellow has been "impressed" by a press gang or impress service, which was limited to seizing men who were, in the broadest sense, seamen. They duly became "imprest" or "prest" men. The word "prest" was a corruption of the French term for "loan."

9 No record of this act has been found. In 1703, an act of Parliament limited the seizure of men to those under eighteen. In 1740, the age was raised to fifty five.

10 The conviction in 1727 of Edmund Curll (1675–1747) for the publication of *Venus in the Cloister* or *The Nun in her Smock* (translated from the French work by Jean Barron, 1683). Under the common law offense of disturbing the king's peace appears to be the first conviction for obscenity in the United Kingdom. Voltaire did not have a copy of this book in his library. By 1728, Thomas Woolston (1670–1733) alone published four *Discourses* on Christ's miracles. He published two further discourses subsequently, but was fined and imprisoned in 1729. Voltaire had copies of all six discourses in his library. (Bibliothèque de Voltaire) (Leningrad, Editions de l'académie des sciences de l'urss, 1961).

11 Although "horse-trading" became synonymous with hard or unfair bargaining later, "horse-fair" was already established as an adjective used attributively to mean "dishonest" or "equivocating." Newmarket remains the home of English racing. See Laura Thompson, *Newmarket: From James I to the Present Day* (London: Virgin Books, 2000).

12 Edward Petre (1631–1699), Jesuit confessor of James II. Voltaire asserts in his history, *Le siècle de Louis XIV*, that, "devoured by the ambition to be cardinal and primate of "England," Petre pushed James II "over the precipice." *Oeuvres historiques*. (Paris: Gallinard, 1957), p.761.

13 Anne Boleyn, Henry VIII's second wife, whom he married in 1533 and beheaded in 1536.

14 Henry VIII was rewarded with the title, "Defender of the Faith" after writing a book against Luther, *Assertio Septum Sacramentorum* (1519).

SELECTED BIBLIOGRAPHY

Studies on Voltaire and the *Lettres Philosophiques*

Barber, W. H. "Voltaire and Quakerism: Enlightenment and the Inner Light." *Studies on Voltaire and the Eighteenth Century* 24 (1963): 81–109.

Cronk, Nicholas. "*The Letters Concerning the English Nation* as an English Work: Reconsidering the Harcourt Brown Thesis." *Studies on Voltaire and the Eighteenth Century* 9 (2001): 226–39.

Gargett, Graham. "Oliver Goldsmith and Voltaire's *Lettres philosophiques*." *The Modern Language Review* 96 (2001): 952–63.

Goldzink, Jean. "La religion des *Lettres philosophiques*: Ou l'art du désordre." *Studies on Voltaire and the Eighteenth Century* 292 (1991): 187–200.

Lee, J. Patrick. "The Unexamined Premise: Voltaire, John Lockman, and the Myth of the *English Letters*." *Studies on Voltaire and the Eighteenth Century* 9 (2001): 240–70.

Tichoux, Alain. "Sur les origines de l'Anti–Pascal de Voltaire." *Studies on Voltaire and the Eighteenth Century* 256 (1988): 21–47.

Wootton, David. "Unhappy Voltaire, or 'I Shall Never Get Over It as Long as I Live.'" *History Workshop Journal* 50 (2000): 137–55.

Eighteenth-Century England and Its Relations with France

Black, Jeremy. *Natural and Necessary Enemies: Anglo-French Relations in the Eighteenth Century*. London: Duckworth, 1986.

Colley, Linda. *Britons: Forging the British Nation 1707–1837*. New Haven: Yale University Press, 2005.

de Beer, Gavin, and André-Michel Rousseau. "Voltaire's British Visitors." *Studies on Voltaire and the Eighteenth Century* 49 (1967).

Langford, Paul. *A Polite and Commercial People: England 1727–1783*. Oxford: Oxford University Press, 1998.

Porter, Roy. *Enlightenment: Britain and the Creation of the Modern World*. London: Allen Lane, 2001.

Tombs, Robert, and Isabelle Tombs. *That Sweet Enemy: The French and the British from the Sun King to the Present*. London: Heinemann, 2006.

Voltaire's Life and Thought

Menant, Sylvain. *L'esthétique de Voltaire*. Paris: Sedes, 1995.

Pearson, Roger. *Voltaire Almighty: A Life in Pursuit of Freedom*. London: Bloomsbury, 2006.

Pomeau, René, *et al. Voltaire en son temps*. 2 vols. Oxford: Voltaire Foundation, 1985.

Trousson, Raymond. *Dictionnaire Voltaire*. Brussels: Hachette, 1994.

Versaille, André, ed. *Dictionnaire de la pensée de Voltaire par lui-même*. Paris: Complexe, 1994.

Other Works by Voltaire

Voltaire. *The Complete Works of Voltaire*. Edited by Theodore Besterman, Geneva and Oxford: Voltaire Foundation, 1968– .

___. *Candide and Related Texts*. Translated and edited by David Wootton. Cambridge, Mass.: Hackett, 2000.

___. *Philosophical Dictionary*. Translated by Theodore Besterman. London: Penguin, 1972.

___. *Political Writings*. Edited by David Williams. Cambridge: Cambridge University Press, 1994.

___. *Treatise on Tolerance*. Edited by Simon Harvey and translated by Brian Masters. Cambridge: Cambridge University Press, 2000.